For Those in Peril

For Those in Peril

The Life and Career of James Holland Walker

Charlie Owen

Troubador Publishing Ltd
Unit E2 Airfield Business Park
Harrison Road, Market Harborough
Leicestershire LE16 7UL
Tel: 0116 279 2299
Email: books@troubador.co.uk
Web: www.troubador.co.uk

ISBN: 9781805144755

British Library Cataloguing in Publication Data.
A catalogue record for this book is available from the British Library.

Printed and bound in Great Britain by 4edge Limited
Typeset in 11pt Minion Pro by Troubador Publishing Ltd, Leicester, UK

Dedicated to my grandsons,

Myles and Rafe

Front cover: James Holland Walker, 13 August 1913, the year he joined White Star Line – Owen family photograph.

Contents

Introduction   ix

Chapter One   1
Chapter Two   4
Chapter Three   12
Chapter Four   20
Chapter Five   27
Chapter Six   41
Chapter Seven   47
Chapter Eight   57
Chapter Nine   72
Chapter Ten   82
Chapter Eleven   90
Chapter Twelve   95

Source Material   101
Acknowledgements   103

Introduction

"SS Baltic – *6 December 1929*

We the cabin passengers on the SS *Baltic desire to place on record our high appreciation of the gallantry and fine seamanship displayed by Mr. J.H Walker, Third Officer, and his Volunteer Crew, who this day risked their lives in effecting the rescue of the Captain and four men from the schooner 'Northern Lights (sic)' who were in the last extremity of distress. We regret with sincere sorrow the loss of the captain's son and hereby express our deep sympathy with him in his sad bereavement."*

Sixty two signatures from a complement of 326 passengers were appended to the bottom of the document that was subsequently given to Captain Davies of the SS *Baltic* and eventually made its way to the offices of the White Star Line in Liverpool. As it later became apparent, many of the witnesses to the rescue of the crew of the schooner *Northern Light* believed they were watching what amounted to a suicide mission. In the prevailing weather conditions, there appeared to be little chance of getting the crew off their stricken vessel and almost none of getting them or their rescuers back onto the *Baltic*.

Yet Walker and his volunteer crew achieved both with the loss of just one unfortunate man from the *Northern Light*. It was an extraordinary act of gallantry and seamanship that would later be recognised by King George V, but it was not the first time that Third Officer James Holland Walker of the White Star Line had undertaken a successful rescue at sea. Nor would it be his last act of bravery in a career in the Merchant Navy that lasted until his retirement in 1947. James Holland Walker was one of a special breed of White Star Line heroes. He was my great-uncle and it is my honour to tell his story.

Charlie Owen
Weymouth – January 2024

Chapter One

The sea is a harsh place to earn a living. In the late nineteenth and early twentieth centuries, death was a regular visitor to the homes of seafarers; not just as a consequence of the appalling infant mortality rates that existed at that time, but as numerous bread winners vanished at sea with their ships. I come from such a family that lived in Liverpool, and a visit from the Grim Reaper in February 1893 led directly to my familial links and to the subject of this story, James Holland Walker.

My great-grandfather, like his father before him, was a mariner. Joseph Pipes Owen was a White Star Line man and that month was serving on board the SS *Naronic* as a ship's carpenter. On the day he sailed, Joseph and his wife Annie had argued and he had left their home at 8 Romeo Street, Toxteth, slamming the door behind him. It was a moment Annie regretted for the rest of her life. The *Naronic* sailed on 11 February 1893, bound for New York, and vanished with all hands.

On 1 July 1893 the publication, *Shipping World* reported:

"All hope of ever hearing any details of the loss of the Naronic has now been abandoned. A fund for the widows and orphans has been started in Liverpool and the White Star Company have found employment for a number of the widows in their works in Bootle in upholstery work, sewing and sail making etc."

Amongst those widows and orphans was my great-grandmother, Annie, and her two children–Mattie, aged nearly eight, and my grandfather Harry, who was eighteen months old. It is not known if they ever benefited from the fund that was set up, but Annie soon took a cleaning job at the docks with the White Star Line. Mattie and Harry were cared for by friends and family. Annie latterly went to sea herself, as a steward on White Star ships. Her time at sea brought her into contact with the man who would become her second husband. Robert Owen (no relation) was an engineer with White Star and he and Annie eventually married on 15 November 1895 in Christ Church, Bootle. Fairly late in life, Annie started a second family, giving birth to three daughters, the youngest being Florence (Florrie) born in 1905.

Around that time, struggling to support a large family, Annie decided that it was time that young Harry should move on. At the age of thirteen he was taken by his mother one evening to a ship docked in the port, where she left him in the care of one of the crew (hopefully someone she knew and trusted). Harry was given a sack to lie on, where he cried himself to sleep. The next morning he sailed as a bellboy on a ship bound for New Orleans. When his colour blindness became apparent and his inability to distinguish red from green rendered him utterly unsuitable to act as a lookout, he undertook a five-year engineering apprenticeship encouraged by his step-father and on 24 February 1913 he joined the White Star Line as an engineer and began a career at sea that would last forty-two years.

That same year, James Holland Walker also joined White Star Line. The two men became lifelong friends, often voyaged together and James (or Jim as he was commonly known) became a regular visitor to the Owen family home at 54 Trinity Road, Bootle, when he was home on leave. There he met Florrie, Harry's half-sister, who he would marry in 1942 towards the end of his career and became inextricably linked to the Owen family. It is a slim link but one I am happy to grasp.

Chapter Two

Hull has long been a large and busy port on the bank of the Humber River. However, the deep-water channel it lies beside did not guarantee its trading position until the 1870s, because the bulk of Hull's steam shipping had the choice of Goole or Grimsby, or even the ports on the north-east coast. Compared to Liverpool, which had little or no competition on the west coast, Hull had competition and was vulnerable.

The industrial development of Hull between 1840 and 1870 was largely driven by the building of the railway between Hull and the West Riding, which opened in July 1840. For the next few years, Hull was riding high on the east coast. The shipping industry in Hull from 1840 onwards showed two very distinctive characteristics which persisted for the next forty years or so. The volume of coastal traffic, as opposed to inland water transport, was not great. Between 1844 and 1845, 425,000 tons of shipping entered and left Hull in the coastal trade compared to 682,000 tons that was dealt with by the much smaller port at Bristol. Secondly, Hull's overseas trade was almost exclusively with the ports of Northern Europe. In 1860, from a total tonnage of 711,00 which came into the port, 554,000 came from Northern Europe.

By the 1870s, trawling was firmly established in Hull. A list of the fishing fleet in 1878 shows seventy-eight smack owners. The bulk of the boats were owned by men who ran one or two boats. Fishing was a brutal but highly paid business but there was widespread anxiety in Hull about the conditions that young boys and apprentices were experiencing. Complaints of widespread brutality at sea, drunkenness and visits to brothels whilst ashore were exacerbated by the practice of recruiting crews directly from any of the numerous workhouses in the city. The murder of two young boys at sea in 1881 and 1882 led to a newspaper campaign and a Board of Trade enquiry that demanded and got, some changes.

Industry in Hull was fairly diversified. Shipping, oil milling, paint manufacture, fishing and cotton manufacture were all substantial employers by the end of the 1870s. In addition, there were numerous ancillary occupations supporting a big port–railway workers, barge and lighter-men, ships chandlers and shipping clerks and agents. There were also the tanners and brewers typical of most large cities at the time. One highly unusual and unexpected industry was the organ factory of Messrs. Forster and Andrews, which between 1864 and 1902 was making, on average, twenty five organs a year for churches in England and abroad.

Because of its widely diverse range of industries, Hull did not suffer the devastating changes of fortune meted out to the single industry towns of Lancashire and the West Riding following the slackness of trade as north-eastern Europe recovered from the effects of the 1841 revolutions, The Crimean War during 1854 -1856 or the cotton famine of 1861–1865. Mass unemployment in Lancashire in 1842 was not mirrored in Hull.

A significant characteristic of industry in Hull was the huge proportion of jobs that were seasonal or casual, and uncertain in their longevity. By 1901, dockers were the largest occupational group in Hull. Their work was usually casual as was the majority of employment in the docks including the seamen because of its reliance on trade with Baltic ports which are frozen shut in winter. By 1885, the population of Hull had grown to just over 186,000. It had grown rapidly after 1870 with the likelihood of overcrowding in limited housing stocks and already inadequate public services. A great deal of the housing in the city would be described as slums.

As a large port, Hull had distinctive sanitary problems. There was the constant risk of epidemics introduced from abroad, made more serious by the shiploads of immigrants arriving in the city, usually on their way to America via Liverpool. Many of the diverse industries that had sprung up in Hull and ensured its survival at times of industrial downturn introduced potentially unsanitary establishments. Fish manure works, slaughterhouses, large numbers of foreign cattle brought in from Europe, soap manufacturers and seed crushing mills all contributed to the toxic mix threatening to engulf the city. All the detritus and waste generated by the city's inhabitants and its businesses made its way along open drains directly into the Humber by gravitation only, with the result that the outfalls into the river were closed by the tides for up to seventeen hours a day. The stench is not hard to imagine.

Few homes had water closets. A privy system with its attendant nuisance of night soil collectors and muck garths remained general except in the newest middle-class housing. Contemporary Public Health investigators were hugely concerned with conditions in the city which, in truth, were no worse than in most other British cities at the time. Identifying the number of different trades in the city as a source of some of the health issues facing its citizens, one investigator wrote in a very understated fashion that, "there is such a quantity of waste matter to be got rid of that the result might easily be less satisfactory than it is". Unquestionably, the issue was exacerbated by the continued practice of converting disused brickyards into building sites and making the foundations for future houses with the refuse. "All the nondescript putrescible organic matter that is to be found in the market, stall, and shop sweepings, kitchen refuse, street scrapings and dust heaps of a great seaport town (conspicuously fish heads and bad oranges) have gone to form the ground on which many of the back streets of Hull are built", wrote the same concerned investigator.

Sanitary improvement in Hull was driven by two crises. The first was a scarlet fever epidemic which killed 689 people in Hull and Sculcoates in 1881. The average age of the dead was less than five years. The epidemic provoked outcry in the city and a government enquiry soon ensured that several necessary improvements were made. Pumps were installed on both the western and eastern drainage systems, eliminating the tides holding the city to ransom each day and pumping its waste into the open sewer that the Humber had become, all day. A new fever hospital was built to replace a ramshackle wooden building, an attempt was made to improve the system of night-soil collection by reducing the number of contractors from fifty-two to nine, a refuse destructor was built, and crucially, the post of Medical Officer of Health and Port Medical Officer was made a full-time one.

The second crisis was more prolonged and serious. Mortality from infantile diarrhoea, impacting largely on children under the age of one, averaged at 237 a year in the 1870s and rose to an annual average of 311 in the first decade of the twentieth century. The worst year was 1911 with 608 infant deaths. It is hard to contemplate the awful conditions and suffering these unfortunate children and their families were enduring. Proposals in 1895/1896 to provide employment for the unemployed in Hull by covering over the open drains that criss-crossed the city came to nothing. Largely, the sanitary conditions of the inner working-class districts of Hull changed little between the 1840s and the outbreak of war in 1914. Life expectancy rates prior to 1914 in Hull were forty-nine years for men, and fifty-three for women.

This was the city that James (Jim) Holland Walker was born into on 1 April 1886. He was born at home, as was the usual practice, at 15 Arthur's Terrace, Barnsley

8

Street in the district of Southcoates. He was the eighth of nine surviving children born to Frederick and Elizabeth Walker between 1877 and 1889. Originally from the Wisbech, Cambridgeshire area, it is assumed Frederick had moved to Hull with Elizabeth soon after their marriage in 1874 in search of work. As was the norm in those days, Elizabeth spent the best years of her life pregnant and raising a large number of children to guard against the ever-present scourge of infant mortality. She clearly lost some children during pregnancy or soon after their birth, but she ensured the survival of nine. Frederick is described variously as a dock gatehand and occasional mariner, clearly taking what employment he could find in the docks. The fate of Jim's siblings is unknown, but I am fairly certain that only Jim followed his father into a career associated with the sea.

Although from an impoverished background, Jim's education was clearly of a decent standard. Certainly sufficient to see him admitted into the famous Hull Trinity House Navigation School in 1897 at the age of eleven. The uniform the pupils wore at the school were almost identical to those worn by the young powder monkeys on Nelson's HMS *Victory*. His route into the highly regarded school was by way of examination. The school records show that he had previously been educated at Crowle Street Boys School and that the Walker family were now living at 14 Sackville Terrace, Ferries Street, Hull. On 23 August 1897, Jim presented himself at the school, took the entrance examination and succeeded in passing, coming twenty-eighth out of a group of thirty successful candidates. Their original numbers had already been thinned out, with eight candidates failing to make the height requirements of 4ft 3inches for boys under twelve years and 4ft 4 inches for boys over that age. A further boy was rejected by the school surgeon when he was found to be shortsighted. On 30 August the successful students for that year's intake met the school committee and on 24 September 1897 Jim commenced his naval education and career under the watchful eye of the wonderfully named headmaster, Zebedee Scaping.

Jim appears to have adapted well to his years at the school. One record for the science examinations in 1899 shows that he obtained a First Class Success in Navigation. As well as that crucial qualification, the students were schooled in mathematics, semaphore, astronomy, boat-work, use of the sextant, compass work and a myriad of other skills required for a life at sea on a sailing ship. On 11 April 1901, Mr. Scaping wrote to the school committee informing them that Jim had consented to join a barque owned by Captain George Mills of Dover and to be bound to him as an apprentice for four years. According to the school's rules, Jim was discharged from the school on 15 April 1901 and subsequently made his way to Dover to commence a career at sea.

Queen Victoria had passed away only a few weeks earlier, aged eighty-one on the Isle of Wight. As Britain and its Empire entered a period of mourning, Jim was on the North Sea. The end of the Victorian era, and the beginning of the Edwardian and Georgian eras, coincided very neatly with his career. It would end forty-six years later in the reign of George VI. He was fifteen years old and could not possibly have imagined what an extraordinary life laid ahead of him.

Chapter Three

The details of Jim's first steps into a life at sea are sketchy at best. Very little confirmed information has been unearthed and I have been largely reliant on a number of typed pages that I came across in the Liverpool Maritime Museum archive that appear to be a record of an interview someone had had with Jim about his career. It has the appearance of research for an article or book about Jim but I cannot say that it ever saw the light of day. The information on those pages suggests that the interview probably took place in around 1954.

His career did not start well! He clearly found life on Captain Mill's barque, *Santon*, very tough, and in his own words he, "went over the side". He then walked from Dover to London with 7d in his pocket, intending to stay with relatives. One of his relatives was apparently a police Superintendent who took a dim view of his absence from his ship and locked him in the police station cells for the night to help him focus on his priorities. It's a colourful story and there is absolutely no way to confirm it but the conclusion to it was that after returning to Hull he came to his senses, walked back to Dover over a period of four days and requested to rejoin his ship. Generously, Captain Mills took him back and he remained on the *Santon* for a period of three years and four months until he was shipwrecked for the first time.

The following passages in this story concerning the five significant events at sea that Jim experienced, have all been given their own What3Words location for reference. What the company concerned has done is to apply to every three-metre-square of the planet a unique combination of three words. Accordingly, my front door has its own three word combination, as does the site of the sinking of the *Santon* and Buckingham Palace. Had What3Words and the internet existed in June 1931, Jim could have navigated his way to the Palace to receive his Sea Gallantry medal from George V using ///fence.gross. bats .

To use this innovation, download the free App and type the three words into the search bar. As the locations in this story are all at sea, it is necessary to reduce the map considerably to get an idea of how remote they are.

Shipwreck of the Santon– 17 January 1904
///bunches.shelter.pillory

On 13 January 1904, the *Santon* left Hull bound for Dover carrying a cargo of gas coal. Very soon the ship encountered appalling weather conditions in the North Sea. Ranging from thick fog through to huge seas and a howling gale, the *Santon* was soon in deep trouble. Still just seventeen years of age, Jim and the other crew were desperately trying to keep their vessel afloat. Waves crashing over the decks soon penetrated into the holds, flooding all compartments.

After taking on water for four days and now in dire straits, salvation arrived on 17 January in the form of the Dutch steamer *Niobe* of the Royal Netherlands Steamship Company out of Amsterdam, under the command of Captain J. Mensick. Displaying exceptional courage and seamanship, Mensick and his crew made three attempts to get the crew of the *Santon* to safety. On the third, Jim and the others were plucked to safety, fed, watered and given dry clothing and eventually taken into Dover, where they made their way to the Dover Sailors' Home. The *Santon* was abandoned to sink in its own time, though an enterprising passing crew picked it up in a derelict and abandoned condition later that month and towed it into Dover as a prize crew. It appears she enjoyed a second life, as in 1911 she was still at sea but owned by a new master, William Slater of Middlesborough.

The rescue of the crew of the *Santon* first came to the attention of the public as the result of a brief news item in the *Shields Daily Gazette* on 18 January. On 19 January the *Liverpool Mercury* reported that, "Lloyds Dover agent telegraphed yesterday 'Captain Mills, master and owner of the barque *Santon* of Liverpool, has been landed this morning with his crew from the Royal Netherlands Steamship Company's steamer *Niobe*, they having abandoned their vessel in a sinking condition at 4pm yesterday (18 Jan) in lat.52 11N, lon.3 *58E*".

The *Dover Express* on 22 January, the *Folkestone Express* and *Sandygate, Shorncliffe and Hythe Advertiser* on 23 January all carried reports, and then in a letter to the *Lloyds List* on 28 January, officialdom stepped in. That letter from W. C. Robinson, His Britannic Majesty's Consul in the British Consulate in Amsterdam, recounted the bravery of Captain Mensick and his crew and expressed his hope that the British Government would recognise their actions. It had the desired effect, and on 20 August 1904, the *Liverpool Echo* reported that Board of Trade Awards had been given to a gallant Dutch crew for saving a Liverpool crew. Captain J. Mensink received a piece of silver, Chief Officer A.J. Graftdyk a binocular case and silver medal, and J. Klipp (sailor), H. de Uries (cook) and G. Ronday (donkeyman) silver medals and money gifts (£3). The *Niobe*, a 654 ton steamer built in 1902, saw subsequent service in World War I, being captured by U-boat 21 in the North Sea on 7 September 1916 before being scuttled at Bruges in 1918 to prevent her falling into allied hands. The fates of Captain Mensink and his gallant crew are unknown. It was apparent though, from the notes of Jim's interview in 1954, that the gallantry of Mensink and his crew had a profound impact on young Jim. I am sure that what he witnessed that day inspired him to become the seaman he did.

Returning to Hull, Jim continued his apprenticeship on numerous ships engaged on both long and short runs. His aspiration at this time was to rise to the position of harbour master at Hull but before long he had decided he wanted to be at sea. He took pretty much any voyage he could find. On one occasion he performed a 'pier-head jump' when the skipper of a departing ship called out for an additional crew member. Volunteering there and then, Jim boarded in his street clothes and by the time his mother arrived at the docks with his sea-going attire his ship was a speck on the horizon. He returned home six months later, having sailed to South America. Back in Hull he took shore jobs before joining the Wilson Line of Hull as a rigger. He began to get the qualifications he would need to become an officer in the Merchant Navy. In 1909 he obtained his Second Mate's Certificate, in 1911 his First Mate's Certificate and finally his Master's Certificate in 1913.

Jim joined the Cunard Line in June 1907 as a substitute Fourth Engineer and was engaged on the *Saxonia* which left Liverpool on 25 June. The *Saxonia* was a passenger and cargo ship, built in 1900 in response to competition from the White Star Line and plied its trade between Liverpool and Boston in the United States. He was now twenty-two years old, a stocky 5ft 6 inches and immensely strong young man, with brown eyes, dark hair and like many of his sea-going contemporaries, sporting tattoos; a mermaid and a pair of clasped hands on his right forearm were probably the result of a youthful, alcohol-fuelled run ashore but they were rarely, if ever, seen. Certainly, my cousin Jennifer who lived close by him in the 1960s never saw them. He gave his address at the time of his engagement as 33 Dale Road, Liverpool and received the princely sum of £9 a week. The balance of pay owed to him when he was discharged in July was £5 19s 7d.

Armed with his Master's Certificate, Jim next took the step that would change his life dramatically and joined the White Star Line on 5 August 1913 as a junior officer. His first appointment was as a Fourth Mate on the *Haverford*, which was largely engaged transporting migrants and cargo to the United States. Amongst his fellow officers on the bridge was none other than Joseph Groves Boxhall, one of the few officers to have survived the sinking of the *Titanic* the year before. Jim and Boxhall (both natives of Hull and graduates of the Hull Trinity House Navigation School) became good friends and over the courses of their careers sailed together many times. When joining the *Haverford* Jim gave his address as 11 Ferries Street, Hull. He was paid £10 a month and on his discharge from the ship in September 1913 his balance of wages was £9 17s 2d.

The enduring tragedy of the White Star Line is that despite everything that it achieved, it is, in the eyes of a large majority, forever only associated with the catastrophe that befell the *Titanic* in 1912. It has become the original metaphor for hubris, arrogance, criminal incompetence, ineptitude and snobbery. Films such as *'Titanic'* by James Cameron have reinforced that view. The reality is that the White Star Line began life in 1845 operating a fleet of sailing clippers that carried passengers and cargo between Britain and Australia and did so very successfully until 1867. That year the Bank of Liverpool failed, leaving White Star with an unmanageable debt of over £500,000, a huge sum then. The company was forced into bankruptcy and its future looked bleak until the flag and name were snapped up by

Thomas Ismay on 18 January 1868. Ismay began to realise his dream of operating a fleet of steam ships and under his leadership the White Star Line quickly became one of the largest, most powerful and successful shipping lines in the world, albeit saddled with enormous debt. Thomas Ismay was succeeded by his son, J. Bruce Ismay, and in 1902 he sold the company to International Mercantile Marine (IMM) headed by J. P. Morgan. Ismay remained as its managing director, and President of IMM. He was vilified after the sinking of the *Titanic* on her maiden voyage, with questions asked often and loudly about his role in the sinking and his perceived cowardice in taking a place on one of the few lifeboats. Pilloried during and after the public enquiry into the disaster, Ismay retired from both White Star and IMM in 1913, the year Jim and my grandfather Harry Owen began their long careers at sea with the company.

The loss of the *Titanic* exercises a macabre hold on the wider public to this day. All things White Star, but particularly *Titanic*, command eyewatering prices. I recognise the lure of the siren voices from the *Titanic*. Whilst I was overjoyed to discover Jim's association with White Star, it was matched by the revelation that a lifelong friend and colleague of his had been Joseph Groves Boxhall, survivor from the *Titanic*. Having expressed that sentiment in black and white, I still cannot fully explain why that should be so significant to me.

Today, restricted at every turn by health and safety regulations, it is difficult to believe what passed for acceptable in designing a ship to cross the North

Atlantic carrying large numbers of human beings. There have been similar and greater losses of life at sea since the sinking of the *Titanic* but none of those events has gripped public imagination and interest in the same way. *Titanic* and the White Star Line are forever synonymous with tragedy.

Chapter Four

The outbreak of hostilities in August 1914 saw Jim spend time between 1914 and 1915 attached to the *Manxman* as a Second Mate. The *Manxman* was largely engaged in moving allied troops across to France. However, by the middle of 1915 he had been transferred to the campaign at Gallipoli and was aboard the *Britannic*, which had been repurposed as a hospital ship, under Captain Bartlett. His role as Second Mate was to coordinate the evacuation of wounded British and Anzac troops from the beaches in the vicinity of Mudros by motorboats.

Granted home leave at the end of 1915, Jim returned to Hull where he married a local girl, Mary Putt Rowse on 11 November at St. Mathews Church. Mary was four years older than Jim, and according to their marriage certificate, they were living next door to each other at 30 and 32 Camden Street, Hull. Witnesses to the marriage were his father Frederick and his elder brother, Jonathan. From Mary's side only her younger sister Milicent, was present. Her mother and other siblings did not attend.

The 1911 census shows Mary living at No. 32 with her

mother and siblings whilst the Walker family are all at 19 Crowle Street, Hull. It was always assumed that Jim had been at sea when the census had been conducted but the marriage certificate clarifies things; Jim, now aged twenty-nine, was living next door to his future wife in Camden Street. The marriage certificate gives Jim's occupation as 'Mercantile Marine', whilst a line has been drawn through Mary's occupation. In 1911 we know that she was single and the manageress of Bazaar Domestic Stores.

The Rowse family were a mariner family originally from Brixham in Devon, who had clearly followed a similar path to Jim's own family and moved to Hull in search of work. Mary's elder brother Charles, who was the same age as Jim, spent his life as a pilot on the Humber river.

After a brief period at home, Jim returned to the *Britannic* for the conclusion of the Gallipoli operation, though he was not on board when the *Britannic* hit a mine off the island of Kea and sank with the loss of thirty lives on 21 November 1916. In 1917 he was appointed as the Gunnery Officer at the height of the German submarine campaign in the Mediterranean, first on the *Canopic* and then the *Ceramic*. On one occasion, Jim and his crew sighted and fired on a submarine at close quarters. The submarine immediately disappeared under water (it was not known if it was hit). For this action he was presented with a cheque by Sir Alfred Yarrow, a first baronet, and founder of the Yarrow shipbuilding dynasty. In January 1918, after eighteen months continuous service in the Mediterranean, Jim suffered a breakdown, and it was decided to repatriate him back to Britain. That was not an easy or straightforward undertaking and involved a lengthy return via the United States on a ship under constant threat of attack by German submarines, exactly the root cause of his breakdown. Arriving in New York, Jim was transferred onto the White Star ship *Cedric* where after loading she sailed to Halifax in convoy and then headed across the Atlantic for Liverpool, carrying a general cargo and troops destined for the battlefields of France.

The rescue of the SS Montreal– 29 January 1918
///rotates.bandwidth.grit

Under the command of a veteran White Star Line Captain, James Oliver Carter for this voyage, the *Cedric* (one of the White Star's Big Four) had had a chequered past involving a number of collisions and mishaps. By the evening of 29 January 1918, *Cedric* had arrived off Morecambe Bay in fine, clear weather. Heading south for Liverpool, she was steaming flat out at around fifteen knots and independently of the convoy she had been part of crossing the Atlantic.

At 2:30pm that day, Canadian Pacific's *Montreal* had left Liverpool bound for Lamlash on the Isle of Arran, carrying a general cargo. About 6:40pm, Captain Arthur Clews, having followed a zig-zag course to counter the submarine threat, sighted the light of a vessel on his port bow approaching at speed. It was the *Cedric*, which, in accordance with Admiralty orders, had been displaying only her stern light until about 6pm when

Carter had sighted the *Montreal* and ordered all lights on. A combination of error and misinterpretation of what both captains were seeing meant that both ships began to turn towards each other. Too late, Carter on the bridge of the *Cedric* recognised the peril they were in and instructed the Second Engineer to reverse both engines, but her stern struck the *Montreal* on her port side abaft the engine room. The *Montreal* was badly damaged by the considerably larger White Star ship and began to take on water. Members of the *Montreal's* crew had been thrown into the sea and there had been two fatalities.

On board the *Cedric*, seeing the plight of men struggling in sea that at that time of the year has an average temperature of seven degrees, Jim and another officer named George Oliver (later Captain Oliver) requested that they be allowed to launch one of the lifeboats to attempt a rescue. Captain Carter agreed and a lifeboat was put into the water. For the second time in his fledgling career, Jim found himself in a lifeboat, albeit this time of his own choosing. Jim and George Oliver began to haul in survivors from the *Montreal*.

However, as the *Cedric's* log would show, events took a turn for the worse:

    6.00pm: Full speed
    6.36pm: Stop and full speed astern
    6.39pm: Stop. Collided with SS *Montreal*
    6.45pm: Put out boat to rescue men in the water
    6.48pm: Slow ahead

6.53pm: Stop

6.55pm: Half and full astern

6.57pm: Stop

7.00pm: Received order from escort to abandon
boat and proceed full speed to destination

7.13pm: Slow ahead

7.25pm: Stop

7.40pm: Notified destroyers of none return of our
boat

7.43pm: Full speed and proceeded

7.50pm: Destroyer signalled we will pick up your
boat

9.37pm: Slow and various (courses) towards Bar.
Lt.V (Light vessel) and anchorage…

Jim, his companion George Oliver, and the survivors from the *Montreal* were now adrift in the freezing dark in the Irish Sea, though thankfully a lot of people knew they were there. The menace of the German submarine fleet had forced the hands of the Admiralty and the convoy commander. By Jim's account, it was several hours before they were plucked out of the sea by the British destroyer HMS *Portia*.

Jim later recounted that his brief trip on board *Portia* into Birkenhead was the only time in his entire career that he was seasick ("blotted his copybook" in his words). Apparently, the motion of a destroyer was completely different to that of a merchant vessel.

The *Montreal* eventually sank fourteen miles from the Barr Lightship and soon after a court case ensued. In

May 1918, *'The Shipping World'* reported, "both steamers were found to blame, but the damage was divided", three-fourths to *Cedric* and one fourth against *Montreal*. On 10 March 1919 the White Star Line were judged to be entitled to limited liability and that "in respect of loss of life caused by improper navigation", they were answerable to damages not exceeding £301,239 15s. Also found liable for the loss of the *Montreal* itself and her cargo, it proved to be an expensive collision for the White Star Line.

It was clearly a collision that none of the parties involved wished to dwell on. Jim and George Oliver's humanitarian actions in launching a lifeboat and rescuing survivors from the *Montreal* received absolutely no official recognition. No mention of the event was made in the British press and in the euphoria following the Armistice in November 1918, the whole matter was quietly forgotten about.

Jim's war was still not quite over. His recuperation at home was distinctly brief. On 7 March 1918 he was engaged on the *Ceramic* as Second Mate and sailed for New York. For the rest of the war, he remained on the *Ceramic*, crossing between Liverpool and New York and was in that city on the day the Armistice was declared. Prior to the Armistice, and clearly sensing future opportunities, he had used his regular visits to New York to study for his United States Master's Certificate. On 3 October 1918 he was awarded his licence number 71684, issued in New York which authorised him to "sail as master of any steam vessel of any gross tonnage upon any ocean", with an added caveat handwritten in red ink that his authority was, "only valid on vessels of the United States requisitioned from foreign lands and for the duration of the present war against the German government". It was valid for five years and enabled Jim to take his place on the SS *Prinz Friedrich Wilhelm*, which was surrendered to the British in March 1919 and transferred to the United States Shipping Board the same month. Jim spent the period between April and August 1919 assisting the United States Navy in returning US troops home from France.

Jim's first world war was over in September 1919. He had acquitted himself well and earned his campaign medals. A quieter life back in the White Star Line family beckoned and with his wartime marriage now in trouble and destined to fail, Jim disappeared on long sea voyages as often as he could.

Chapter Five

The 1920s and 1930s were boom years for the wealthy classes of Britain, Europe, and the United States, the 'Bright Young Things' as they were known by the tabloid press of the day. Ocean travel between the United States and Europe became big business with the various shipping companies vying constantly to be the biggest and fastest to and from those continents. There was fierce competition and public interest in the Blue Riband for the fastest Atlantic crossing. Cunard was the most regular holder of the award, with the *Queen Mary* being the last Cunarder to hold it. The SS *United States* took the record in 1952 and holds it to this day.

It appears that Jim probably made Liverpool his adopted home towards the end of the 1910s. The city was not dissimilar to the city of his birth, Hull. Enormous wealth at one end of the scale, abject poverty at the other. Low life expectancy, rampant infant mortality, and appalling public sanitation and living conditions for many, all mirrored life in Hull in the late nineteenth century. Throughout the nineteenth century the city's trade and population boomed. Huge growth in the cotton trade and the development of trading links with India and the Far East required the construction of more and bigger docks. Between 1824 and 1858, 140 acres of new docks and ten miles of extra quay space were built. The population growth Liverpool experienced owed much to trade but also to the disaster unfolding in Ireland during the Great Famine between 1845 and 1849. In 1847 alone, nearly 300,000 people arrived in Liverpool from Ireland and by 1851 nearly 25% of the town's population had originated from Ireland. There were other communities taking root in Liverpool as well. Between 1851 and 1911, at least 20,000 people from Wales arrived in the town, every decade. Those numbers peaked in the 1880s, the decade that my great-grandfather left North Wales and settled in Liverpool. Liverpool was sometimes referred to as the capital of North Wales.

The area of Gerard, Hunter, Lionel and Whale Streets, off Scotland Road, attracted so many Italian immigrants that it became known as Little Italy. The town's Chinatown is believed to be the oldest and largest Chinese community in Europe. Liverpool was granted city status in 1880 and by 1901 its population had expanded to over 700,000. By 1916 the three pierhead buildings (the Three Graces), including the Liver building, had been erected and as the city prospered it regarded itself as the 'Second City of the Empire'. Despite the wealth flowing into and out of the city, there continued to be extreme poverty. My late father recalled being taken to play football in a local park by his father home on leave in the early 1930s and being encouraged to share his football with a group of other boys who were barefooted, unwashed, and wearing threadbare clothes. His father had experienced a tough childhood in the city and was keen that his youngest son should understand his own good fortune.

Liverpool's history as a major slave port in the eighteenth and early nineteenth centuries is a dreadful stain on its reputation, though even in a city so entrenched in the trade there were vocal abolitionists. Whilst barbarians such as the local MPs Richard Pennant, Bamber Gascoyne and Banastre Tarleton were noisy supporters of the trade (in 1789, speaking against William Wilberforce's efforts to abolish slavery, Pennant told the House of Commons that "if they passed the vote of abolition they actually struck at seventy millions of property, they ruined the colonies and by destroying an essential nursery of seamen, gave up the dominion of the sea at a single glance"), there were other, more enlightened and humane inhabitants. William Roscoe and Henry Brougham were ardent opponents of the evil trade and instrumental in bringing about its abolishment in 1807. But it took time. Slavery in the British colonies was only finally abolished in 1833 and replaced with 'apprenticeships' which existed until 1838 when they too were abolished. The abolishment was no kind of benevolent act. On the contrary, British slave owners were handsomely compensated by the government for their lost slaves. Slavery continued illicitly with slavers supplying the markets in Brazil and elsewhere; a ship carrying slaves was recorded leaving Liverpool as late as 1862. It is estimated that around 1.5 million enslaved

Africans passed through Liverpool en route to the British colonies and the Americas.

Jim now began to cross the Atlantic regularly and travel to New Zealand on a number of White Star ships. September 1919 saw him on the *Baltic* and living in Liverpool at 14 Royton Road. By now he appears to have made the city his adopted home and thereafter there is little, if any, reference to his city of birth. From 1921 he sailed often on the *Olympic*, the *Arabic*, the *Shannonmede*, back on the *Baltic*, the *Georgic*, the *Andania*, the *Acquitania*, the *Berengaria*, the *Franconia*, the *Antonia*, the *Laurentic*, the *Ausonia*, the *Aurania*, the *Bronte* and the *Thermistocles*; but in March 1927 he commenced a voyage from Wellington, New Zealand back to London via Southampton on the *Ionic* that would result in the name of James Holland Walker coming to the attention of the wider public for the first time.

The rescue of the Daisy – 15 April 1927
///earwig.slashing.translation

The *Daisy* was a three-masted, wooden-hulled, 346 ton French schooner from the port of Saint-Malo on the French Atlantic coast. Under the command of Captain Couchard, it had a total crew of twenty-four. Early in April 1927 the *Daisy* had left its home port bound for the plentiful fishing grounds of the Newfoundland Banks. The trip had started badly. Within a few days, in poor weather, a crewman had fallen from the rigging and been lost overboard. Couchard and his vessel returned to Saint-

Malo to recruit a replacement before setting off again on 8 April and into the teeth of a North Atlantic storm. By 10 April the *Daisy* was leaking badly and by 13 April it had become so serious that Couchard requested the assistance of a passing French vessel. That vessel escorted them for the next twenty-four hours, but the skipper deemed the *Daisy* was not in immediate danger and left the stricken vessel to fend for itself. The weather conditions worsened, as did the condition of the *Daisy* and her desperate crew. They had been pumping water constantly for four days and had had no sleep and little food or water. By now, flying flags of distress, the crew of the *Daisy* were not a little pleased to sight the White Star Line ship *Ionic* appear about 6:30pm on Good Friday 15 April 1927.

The *Ionic* was a steam-powered ocean liner built in 1902 by Harland and Wolff in Belfast. Just over five hundred feet in length and weighing a little over 12,000 tons, her quadruple-expansion steam engines and twin-screw propellers could get her up to fourteen knots. With a passenger capacity of 688, she was the second White Star Line ship to carry the name and served the United Kingdom to New Zealand route via Cape Town. She was also the first White Star ship on the New Zealand run to be equipped with wireless.

Captain Alex Jackson did not delay and dispatched Jim (now a Third Officer) and Fifth Officer, Lieutenant W.T Poustie, RNR, to take charge of two lifeboats of volunteer crewmen to get the crew of the *Daisy* off their sinking vessel and onto the *Ionic* and safety. Jim took the first lifeboat away at 7:02pm and he boarded the *Daisy* alone soon after. Managing to converse with Captain Couchard, he quickly established that the *Daisy* was finished and signalled accordingly by lamp to the *Ionic*. At 7:20pm the second lifeboat under Fifth Officer Poustie was launched. The French crew were placed into the two lifeboats whilst Jim, Poustie and Captain Couchard remained briefly on board. The *Daisy* had become a dangerous wreck in the middle of busy shipping lanes in the dark and Captain Couchard agreed that she should be sunk. A 90lb cask of gunpowder was found, placed in the wheelhouse, the woodwork doused with petrol and the fuse lit. The three men quickly returned to the lifeboats to get back to the *Ionic*.

There are two versions of what happened next. In one very colourful account that appeared in 1938 in the *Natal Daily News* as part of an interview with Jim about his career, the strong wind caused the fuse on the gunpowder keg to burn faster than expected and the keg ignited with the lifeboats still alongside. By a miracle, all the occupants were unhurt. A far more restrained and likely account was given later by Captain Jackson, in which he reported that everyone was back on board and the *Ionic* was underway when a huge explosion destroyed the *Daisy* at 8:55pm, leaving nothing but some floating wreckage. Captain Jackson's entry in the *Ionic*'s log is brief:

"6.30pm 15.4.27. 45.2.11.16. Observed signals of distress from French schooner Daisy. 6.38pm stopped and sent away boat in charge of Third Officer. Ascertained schooner was sinking and crew

wished to abandon ship. 8.53pm rescued crew of 24 men and set fire to schooner, destroyed after part of schooner by gunpowder explosion. Reported same to Lloyds."

The *Ionic* then proceeded for Southampton and, using the new wireless, informed the White Star Line of what had occurred. That message generated an article in *The London Times* on 18 April that reported:

"Twenty four members of the crew of the French schooner Daisy who were rescued in the Atlantic as they were preparing to abandon the ship on the evening of Good Friday, were landed at Southampton yesterday. Captain Couchard said that shortly after the schooner left St Malo for Newfoundland one of the crew fell from the rigging and was drowned so that they had to return to port for a substitute. They started again on April 8 and soon encountered a heavy sea. The vessel rolled heavily and strained badly and on the 10th it began to leak. By the 13th their position was very serious and they asked for help from a French vessel which escorted them during the next day. Her captain said that he did not think that they were in immediate danger and left them. Their position got worse and for four days they were continuously at the pumps trying to keep the water down. They were all exhausted when the Ionic came to their rescue. Captain A.E. Jackson of the Ionic said they

found the schooner in a sinking condition. The crew had prepared to leave her. They were in a very bad state having had no sleep and very little food for four days during which they had manned the pumps continuously. As the sinking schooner was in the direct track of liner traffic it was decided it would be better to sink her."

Another three articles in the French newspaper *L'Ouest-Eclair* on 17, 18 and 21 April carried similar accounts. Soon after, official recognition of the rescue followed. The Eighty Eighth Annual Report for the year ended 1 July 1927 of the Liverpool Shipwreck and Humane Society records that:

"Silver medal and Certificate of Thanks each to 3rd officer J.H. Walker and 5th officer Lieut W.T. Poustie, RNR, in charge of the two lifeboats, for praiseworthy and humane service in rescuing the crew (24) of the French schooner 'Daisy' which was abandoned in the North Atlantic in a sinking condition on the 15th April 1927."

Jim and Poustie had been awarded the Bramley-Moore medal for Saving Life at Sea and illuminated certificates of thanks, but the volunteer crewmen who had powered the lifeboats through the pounding waves apparently received nothing.

The French government also saw fit to recognise Jim's role in rescuing their citizens. In June 1928 at Liverpool

Town Hall, Jim was presented with the French Marine Marchande Medal of Honour by Commodore C.A. Bartlett (his captain on the *Britannic* during the Gallipoli campaign) on behalf of the French government. It was accompanied by an illuminated certificate.

It is not known if Poustie was honoured by the French but it is likely that he was. The accompanying photograph captioned 'New Zealanders–*Ionic* 1924' is interesting and raised my hopes that it included some of the men who accompanied Jim in a later rescue, whose names are known. Jim is in his tropical white uniform on the far right. Of the seamen with him, I recognise at least four who appear in photographs with him in 1929 and 1931 in connection with another rescue undertaken by the crew of RMS *Baltic* and discussed later in this book.

Alas, scrutiny of the *Ionic* crew list for the 1927 rescue reveals that none of the men that took part in the 1929 rescue were on board and could not have been in the lifeboats that day. The names of those brave men appear to have been lost.

I have been unable to obtain any information about Captain Couchard and his crew. I am constantly struck by the apparent tender ages of the three young boys sitting at the front of the group. Most likely dead now, surely, they will have surviving relatives who will recognise them?

The rescue of the Northern Light – 6 December 6 1929
///irate.flaked.halving

On the evening of 29 November 1929, a flotilla of eleven

small fishing schooners left the Newfoundland port of St John's, bound for various destinations. For the crews of those ships, the future was uncertain. As recently as October, the world stock markets had crashed, bringing the hedonistic roaring twenties to a screeching halt and threatening the livelihoods of all the men on board. Amongst those small ships was the *Northern Light*, owned and skippered by forty-eight year old Thomas Parsons. Parsons and his family came from the area of Chandlers Reach in the central part of Bonavista Bay, and it was for there that he headed that evening.

Plummeting fish prices were rumoured to be about to drop further, and already at barely break-even point, Parsons knew he would have to get any future provisions on credit. The vicious financial cycle threatened to finish him and he decided to head for home with a mixed cargo of eighty tons made up of molasses, cereals, oil, other staples, and a selection of Christmas toys that he knew would sell well on their return to Bonavista Bay.

The *Northern Light* was a seventy-two foot, wooden-hulled, two-masted schooner built in 1896. Purchased by Parsons in 1909, she was a well-tried and trusted vessel and his crew for that journey home included his two elder sons, Rex aged twenty and Peter aged just eighteen. Three other men also from the Bonavista Bay area, Carty Halloway, Fred Wiseman, and First Mate Richard 'Dick' Russell made up the rest of the crew.

Parsons had serious concerns about the weather with the pressure dropping. However, seeing the other vessels departing St John's, he ignored his gut feeling and years of experience and ordered the *Northern Light* out of the safety of the harbour. The flotilla of eleven ships were all heading north into one of the worst North Atlantic storms in living memory that even today is recalled amongst the seafaring communities of Newfoundland as The Gale of 1929.

Within a few hours he was bitterly regretting leaving St John's. The temperature had dropped along with the pressure and occasional snow flurries carried on a gale-force wind in a sea that was becoming mountainous soon had the exposed crew on the open deck soaked and shivering. Rex Parsons was already extremely unwell with the early symptoms of a bout of pneumonia and his father tried to encourage him to get what shelter he could below deck; but Rex would not hear of it. He saw his place with the rest of the crew battling the elements. The *Northern Light's* journey home was a little over ninety miles and would usually all be within sight of land, but Captain Parsons now realised that the hurricane wind that battered his small ship was very likely to drive them well away from the coast, so he ordered the sails to be close-hauled so that the wind met the sail at an acute angle. It was not enough.

The wind continued to tear across Placentia Bay and threatened to rip away the foresail. As the crew struggled to free the frozen sail, another huge gust ripped the sail away as the boom snapped and the sail disappeared over the side of the ship. The mainsail, despite being close-hauled, was now threatening to either tear to pieces or worse, to capsize the ship. Working feverishly, the crew managed to get it down and the *Northern Light* tilted back to a safer level, but without sails Parsons now had virtually no rudder control. The unrelenting gale carried the small ship away from the lights on the coast and deep into the stormy North Atlantic. The crew were soaking wet, freezing cold, their meagre rations ruined and there was little drinking water. Rex's health continued to worsen. They had no control of their ship and their chances of surviving the storm were diminishing by the minute. The only glimmer of hope was that the storm was driving the *Northern Light* into the main transatlantic shipping lanes. The crew began to fight for their lives.

On the evening of 30 November 1929, the day after *Northern Light* had left St John's, the White Star Line RMS *Baltic* left her moorings in Liverpool and headed along the River Mersey towards the open sea and a passage to New York. The *Baltic*, built in 1904, was another one of the so-called 'Big Four' of the White Star fleet, and whilst she was getting on in age now, she was still a magnificent ship designed specifically to deal with the worst excesses of the North Atlantic weather. Previously under the command of Captain Edward Smith who had gone down on the *Titanic's* maiden voyage, this trip found her under the control of an experienced White Star veteran captain, Evan Davies. By a quirk of fate, the *Baltic* had been in the North Atlantic on 12 April 1912 and had sent warnings of ice to Smith on the *Titanic*. The messages had not been acknowledged. Davies had not been scheduled to command the *Baltic* on this voyage. The original crew list shows Captain J. Kearney as master, but a line has been drawn through the 'Reports for Ability and General Conduct' and an additional entry on the list dated 27 November 1929 records that he had been suspended. A ships log entry on the day they sailed made by Davies records that, "James Kearney, master, superseded. Charts, instruments and all navigating controls handed over to E Davies who was placed on the ships register". The story behind this change of masters is unknown.

The crew list for the voyage also includes a bugler to summon passengers to their meals and lifeboat stations, an interpreter and a five-piece band! Amongst his officers on the bridge that evening were Jim as his Third Officer and his good friend Joseph Boxhall as Second Mate. Jim had only joined the *Baltic* the day she sailed, having travelled up to Liverpool from London where he had left the *Ionic* on 26 November on her return from a trip to New Zealand. It was a very clear example of his desire to be at sea as often as possible.

As the *Baltic* passed Birkenhead she began to feel the force of the gale sweeping across the Atlantic, then turned south, passing Holyhead on her port side, steamed down St George's channel, rounded Cape Clear and after calling briefly at Cobh on 1 December to load more passengers, headed into the North Atlantic. The full force of the storm hit her. Despite her huge size (729 feet long and nearly 24,000 gross tons) Captain Evans quickly realised that he would need to nurse her through the tempest. Ordering 'slow ahead', the *Baltic* began to plough through huge waves as Evans tried to make conditions for his 326 passengers more bearable. By 5 December the *Baltic* had endured a constant battle with the west-northwest gale for almost five days. Hundreds of miles behind her, the storm reached England with extraordinary tides reported along the English Channel coast and the lowlands of the River Thames flooding inland as far as two miles. Seawater flooded over Thames wharves and small buildings were swept away. Evans and his officers had remained on the bridge for almost the whole time, taking only brief periods of rest off watch. Any sleep on board the *Baltic* was well-nigh impossible as even that vast, specially designed, vessel pitched and rolled in twenty foot waves. Virtually all her passengers were now very seasick.

Chapter Six

The twelve line entry in the *Baltic's* logbook on 6 December is brief, to the point and absolutely what you would expect to see, but it completely fails to convey the drama, gallantry and tragedy that unfolded when the *Baltic* and the *Northern Light* happened upon each other quite by chance as it began to get light. Made at 10:10am, probably by the Purser, Mr. R. Edwards, it was signed by Captain Davies and his Chief Mate, Mr. J. H. Jones.

"Sighted Schooner Northern Light flying distress signals in sinking condition. Lowered No.10 lifeboat in charge of J H Walker, 3rd mate and nine men who went to the rescue. Lifeboat returned with the Master and four men: Tom Parsons, Master, Frederick Wiseman, Richard Russell, Peter Parsons, Carty Halloway, Deck Hands. One member of the Schooner's crew was drowned whilst going from the schooner to the Life Boat, he was Rex Parsons aged 20 (son of the Master). The Life Boat crew and survivors were brought aboard the Baltic and we proceeded 11:46am."

The crew of the *Northern Light* had been alerted to the possible presence of the *Baltic* and rescue by the stricken

Rex Parsons who, venturing on deck from his sickbed below, thought he had spotted a light in the north-west. None of the others had seen it and nothing could be seen now. However, a few minutes later, young Peter Parsons shouted that he could see a huge ship; it was the *Baltic*, still some way off and apparently unaware of the presence of the *Northern Light*. The stroke of luck Tom Parsons and his crew had desperately needed had presented itself and he was not about to miss his chance.

He dispatched Carty Halloway below deck to fetch a blanket and a black kettle which he instructed Halloway to tie to the mainmast as he would a flag and to run the strange combination to the top of the mast. Soon the blanket straightened in the gale and the kettle was swinging madly from its handle in the centre. The crew of the *Northern Light* now peered intently in the direction of the big ship, praying that their improvised distress signal would be spotted.

On board the *Baltic*, Captain Davies had retired to his cabin for a brief rest after spending the night on his bridge nursing his ship through the storm. He had barely laid his head on his pillow before he was summoned back to the bridge by Chief Mate Jones with the news that they had sighted an apparently abandoned schooner about five hundred yards away on a bearing of 356 degrees off the port bow. Peering through his binoculars, Davies eventually spotted the *Northern Light* settled deep between two huge waves and immediately recognised an old sailors' improvised flag of distress, a square with a ball hanging from it, flying from the mast of the little schooner.

Ordering the *Baltic* to port, he pointed his ship towards the now jubilant crew on the stricken *Northern Light*.

Captain Davies brought the *Baltic* to within two hundred yards of the *Northern Light*, keeping her to windward to shelter the small schooner as best as he could. Hundreds of the *Baltic's* passengers now lined the railings, alerted to the drama unfolding by the ship's sudden change of direction. From the bridge deck Davies called down to the *Northern Light*, confirmed they had no means of saving themselves (their lifeboat had suffered serious damage during the storm) and told the crew to stand by to be rescued. He then ordered 150 gallons of cod liver oil to be poured into the sea in the hope that it might calm the churning waves and called for volunteers to man a lifeboat to undertake the rescue.

Jim and nine members of the crew stepped forward: John Fitzgerald (Boatswains Mate), John Boylan (Chief Petty Officer), John Whelan (Storekeeper), Peter Codd, William Henry Williams (Quarter Masters), Albert Edward Cole, George Delahay, George Augustus Riley (Able Seamen) and John Roberts (Sailor), donned rudimentary life jackets and some oilskins and climbed aboard Lifeboat Number 10. Other crew then assisted to lower the lifeboat down to the sea as the *Baltic* rode the huge waves with a very real risk that the lifeboat might be dashed to pieces against the hull. Eventually safely delivered to the sea, the nine crewmen began to power their boat away from the *Baltic* using only the strength in their arms. It was an impressive feat of strength and determination but combined with Jim's seamanship the lifeboat was manoeuvred to within a few feet of the stern of the *Northern Light*. Both vessels were being rocked violently to and fro, and only Jim's skill on the rudder and his instructions to his oarsmen prevented the lifeboat being crushed against the schooner. It became obvious that the crew could not be taken off directly and that it would require them to jump into the sea and be pulled out. A daunting prospect at the best of times but particularly so as only Rex and Peter Parsons could swim. It was the only option and bringing the lifeboat to about twenty feet of the stern of the *Northern Light*, Jim threw a line to the waiting crew. They were instructed to tie the rope firmly around their waists, remove their heavy waterproof wet-weather gear and boots, jump in and be pulled into the lifeboat.

Peter Parsons went first and was successfully pulled into the lifeboat. Fred Wiseman and Carty Halloway followed without issue and then Richard 'Dick' Russell stepped up to take his turn. As he paused to better time his jump according to the huge swell, the bow of the lifeboat and the stern of the *Northern Light* almost touched. Seizing his opportunity, Russell jumped directly into the safety of the lifeboat. He landed alongside Jim, slapped him on the shoulder remarking that he had 'come in good time' and then produced a cigarette that he managed to light in the gale with a match that had also remained dry. As each man reached safety, cheers went up from the watching *Baltic* passengers and crew.

Now only Tom and Rex Parsons remained to be saved. Rex's health had continued to worsen and he had been observed laughing deliriously as he had watched his mates being hauled into the lifeboat. He had possibly started to hallucinate. He stepped up to the stern, tied the rope around his waist and without a word to his anxious father, jumped into the sea. He had not tied the rope securely, nor had he removed his heavy seaboots as instructed. He was seen to surface briefly, the rope detached from his body and then his seaboots filled with water. In his weakened condition he was doomed and he disappeared into the depths of the Atlantic. The hundreds of spectators on the *Baltic*, the crew of the lifeboat and the survivors of the *Northern Light* looked on in mute horror.

It took almost twenty minutes for Jim to persuade the stunned Tom Parsons to leave the *Northern Light*. He was observed shouting and banging the railings with his hands, utterly inconsolable, before Jim could get through to him. He eventually jumped and was recovered safely and the lifeboat began the perilous journey back to the *Baltic*, the only sound being Jim's words of command.

The journey back took the best part of three quarters of an hour before Jim got the lifeboat alongside the *Baltic*. There the survivors and Jim's crew were hauled aboard by lines; last on board was Jim himself. Very soon after returning, numerous photographs were taken of the rescued seamen and their rescuers. Understandably, there is an air of relief and euphoria amongst the group of men who have endured and survived significant trauma. All save Tom Parsons, who is quite clearly deeply traumatised and not really present. He was photographed wearing an overcoat and felt hat given to him by one of the *Baltic's* passengers and he stares unseeing at the camera. His face says it all. He has quite literally, lost everything. Expecting his voyage home to Bonavista Bay to take only a few hours, he had anticipated that his insurance on the *Northern Light* and its cargo would be valid for the duration of his voyage. In fact, it had expired whilst they drifted helplessly in the teeth of the gale. He was financially ruined and to put a tin hat on the disaster, he had lost his son Rex. Taken under the protective wing of Captain Davies, he was a broken man. He recovered sufficiently to discuss with Davies his voyage and the location he had been rescued from and was staggered to learn that he was over four hundred miles off his intended course. The odds against the *Baltic* and *Northern Light* encountering each other in the middle of the Atlantic were astronomical. He and his surviving crew were very lucky men, though it was unlikely that anyone thought it appropriate to mention that to him. Captain Davies could not safely recover Lifeboat 10, so it was cast adrift within sight of the *Northern Light*. It is likely that both vessels and young Rex Parsons subsequently lay close to each other. That somehow seems fitting.

*Hull Trinity House school boy, 1868
(Hull Trinity House School)*

*Street plan showing Arthur's Terrace,
Hull, c1880 (Hull History Centre)*

*...oys learning
...emaphore –
...Hull Trinity
...hool, c1880
...Hull Trinity
...use School)*

RMS *Britannic* as a hospital ship
at Mudros, c1915
(Imperial War Museum)

*Harry Owen, Jim's best friend
and the author's grandfather,
c1916 (Owen family)*

*Jim (far right) with crew
members of the Ionic, c1924
(Liverpool Maritime Museum)*

RMS Baltic, c1930 (Owen family)

Jim (far right), Lt Poustie (far left), Captain Jackson (centre) with the rescued crew of the Daisy, 15 April 1927 (Liverpool Maritime Museum)

Jim (front left) with Captain Jackson, Lt Poustie and Captain Couchard and senior crew – Ionic 15 April 1927 (Liverpool Maritime Museum)

Taken from the deck of the Baltic, 6 December 1929. Captioned on rear – taken at a height of 70 ft (Liverpool Maritime Museum)

Lifeboat 10 approaches the stern of the Northern Light, 6 December 1929 (Liverpool Maritime Museum)

Jim (centre) with the survivors of the Northern Light, 6 December 1929 (Liverpool Maritime Museum)

Jim (third from the right) with the men of Lifeboat 10, 6 December 1929 (Liverpool Maritime Museum)

Jim (far right), Captain Davies (far left) with the members of Lifeboat 10 and the survivors of the Northern Light. Skipper Tom Parsons, seated front left, wearing an overcoat and felt hat, 6 December 1929 (Liverpool Maritime Museum)

Jim (in uniform) with 5 members of Lifeboat 10 – Buckingham Palace, 26 June 1931 (Liverpool Maritime Museum)

Cabin class passengers with Jim – Baltic, 6 December 1929 (Liverpool Maritime Museum)

Jim (far right) with 2 unknown officers – Buckingham Palace, 26 June 1931 (Liverpool Maritime Museum)

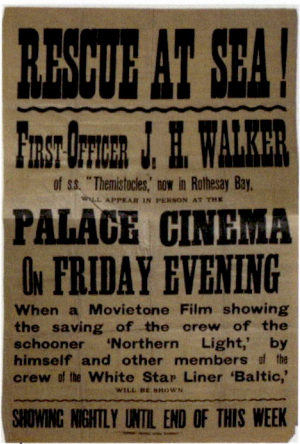

Poster advertising a talk by Jim c1930 (Liverpool Maritime Museum)

Jim enjoying the company of dancing girls, c1930s (Liverpool Maritime Museum)

Jim with more dancing girls! c1930s (Liverpool Maritime Museum)

Ship in a bottle believed to be the Santon (Owen family)

RMS *Ionic* c1925 (Wikipedia)

RMS *Laconia* c1940 (Owen family)

U506 with lifeboat full of survivors (Horst Bredow – U-Boot-Archiv, Cuxhaven)

Laconia survivors on board U506 (Horst Bredow – U-Boot-Archiv, Cuxhaven)

Laconia survivors on U506 with U156 in the background (Horst Bredow – U-Boot-Archiv, Cuxhaven)

Laconia survivors on the deck of U156 (Horst Bredow – U-Boot-Archiv, Cuxhaven)

Laconia survivors being transferred between U506 and U156 (Horst Bredow – U-Boot-Archiv, Cuxhaven)

Admiral Karl Donitz c1944 (Horst Bredow – U-Boot-Archiv, Cuxhaven)

Commander Erich Würdemann (U507) c1941 (Horst Bredow – U-Boot-Archiv, Cuxhaven)

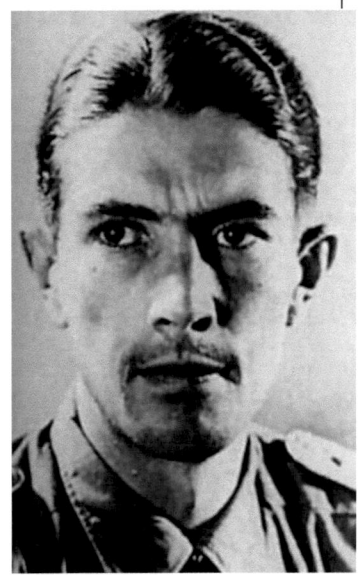

Commander Harro Schacht (U506) c1941 (Horst Bredow – U-Boot-Archiv, Cuxhaven)

Commander Werner Hartenstein (U156) c1941 (Horst Bredow – U-Boot-Archiv, Cuxhaven)

What3Words map showing the site of the Northern Light rescue, 6 December 1929 (W3W/Google maps)

What3Words map showing the site of the Laconia sinking, 12 September 1942 (W3W/Google maps)

What3Words map showing the site of the Santon sinking, 17 January 1904 (W3W/ Google maps)

What3Words map showing the site of the Daisy rescue, 15 April 1927 (W3W/ Google maps)

What3Words map showing the site of the Montreal rescue, 29 January 1918 (W3W/ Google maps)

"Garth", 6 Coronation Drive, Crosby,
June 2023 (Owen family)

Rex Parsons's memorial plaque, 2023
(Parsons family)

Frederica de Laguna, c1929
(Wikipedia)

Brenda Dean Paul, c1925
(Wikipedia)

Jim and his dog Tina at home, c1960 (Owen family)

Joseph Groves Boxhall – Titanic survivor and shipmate, c1913 (Wikipedia)

Jim (far left) with Florrie immediately to his left at a social event in Liverpool,
c1950 (Owen family)

Chapter Seven

Whilst the survivors of the *Northern Light* were treated by the ship's surgeon, J. D. Smylie, the *Baltic* made for New York. News of their rescue of the crew of the *Northern Light* preceded them. One of the cabin-class passengers, Arthur Brewster, forty-four years old from Purley in Surrey, who was travelling with his wife, had observed the entire rescue from the deck and sent a wireless message to an unknown recipient in New York. Brewster was one of the signatories on the letter of condolence. Sent on the day of the rescue, he had a remarkable amount of information about all parties involved, including details of Jim's 1927 rescue of the crew of the *Daisy*. Brewster provided a highly detailed account of the rescue to his correspondent that would subsequently form the basis of numerous newspaper accounts in the United States and back in the United Kingdom. Brewster's occupation is listed on the passenger manifest as 'Manager', obviously a wealthy one, and he clearly had a journalist's nose for what constitutes a story. He was a regular traveller on White Star ships to New York, often continuing on to Canada and usually carried $1,000 with him.

Also on-board was Lt Guy Herbert Major, RNR, who having landed at New York, on 11 December, forwarded a report of the rescue to The Navigators and General Insurance Society, London EC. Jim was apparently a member of the N&G and Major was keen that they heard of their member's gallantry. Major describes in his report that he had watched the rescue with a master mariner and states that he and his companion were of the opinion:

"...that such a feat (with reference to the entire boarding evolution) was well nigh impossible owing to the state of the sea and weather conditions. Once whilst the boat was proceeding to the schooner and once whilst it was returning, it drifted to windward of the parent ship. On both these occasions they were in an extremely critical position and it was only owing to the skill of Mr Walker that both the rescuers and rescued survived."

He finished his report with a paragraph that undoubtedly started a process that ended with Jim and his gallant crew being decorated at Buckingham Palace.

"Having been in conversation with Mr Walker some time after usual routine was resumed, it appears that he was fully awake to the state of affairs, and it seems obvious to me that his cool management and leadership was the true form of heroism."

Lt Major's reference to his companion watching the

rescue with him was added to after he had typed his report to N&G. The words 'master mariner' were inserted by hand. The master mariner in question was Captain John Halliday Murdoch, thirty-nine years, of the Pacific Steam Navigation Company (PSNC) in Liverpool, who was making his way to New York to join his ship, the SS *Arana*. He was among a group of mariners from the PSNC with sequential tickets (including Lt Major) making their way to New York to join PSNC ships. A Scotsman from Dalbeatie, he had been born in Kirkcudbright into a famous seafaring family. His grandfather and father had been captains, and his uncle William had been one of the many officers lost on the *Titanic*. It is believed that Captain Murdoch died at sea aboard his ship in around 1943 but the circumstances are unknown.

Another very interested spectator was Mr. P.A.S. Franklin, President of the International Mercantile Marine Company, the owners of the White Star Line, travelling with his wife. Interviewed about the incident soon after his arrival in New York, Franklin described Jim's performance as the finest seamanship he had ever seen:

> *"We were all intensely interested in getting those poor men to a place of safety. At first it looked as if the rescue could not be accomplished, but when we observed the skill and coolness with which Captain Davies and Walker approached their task, we took heart and had the satisfaction later of seeing a display of seamanship typical of the best traditions of the sea. For unison it could not be*

matched. There was no hitch; no lost time, no lost movement. Every man that had a job to do worked in harmony with his mates. I am extremely proud of Captain Davies, Mr Walker, the sturdy men in the lifeboat and all who participated in the rescue and subsequent care of the shipwrecked men."

Regrettably, I cannot put names that we know to the faces of those 'sturdy men in the lifeboat' shown in the photograph taken on the deck of the Baltic, but the crew manifest gives some assistance by recording the ages of the men when they joined the ship. With the recognition of Mr. Franklin, the bravery of all the men in Lifeboat 10 would subsequently be properly recognised, unlike the crews of the lifeboats launched from the *Ionic* by Jim and Lt. Poustie in 1927.

The London Times carried an extensive account of the rescue, which it had obtained from the family of another of the cabin-class passengers who had witnessed it. Ernest Paul Ortweiler was a twenty-six year old manufacturer from London NW6 who had written to his parents on arrival in New York and provided a graphic account of what he had seen. *The Times* appears to have reprinted his letter almost verbatim. Ortweiler had clearly been close to the action as he described:

"...buckets of oil poured into the waters (and also over the Third Officer who made some audible comments about it in nautical language)."

Ortweiler knew that Jim already held two medals for

saving life at sea and described his crew of nine volunteers as comprising:

> "...*every conceivable type in age from 15 to 50, and in shape as varied as the human form allows; but one was full of admiration for their stout hearts (they knew they hadn't much chance of getting back)*."

The return to the Baltic generated much angst in Ortweiler who recorded:

> "...*for a quarter of an hour my heart never left my mouth. There was hardly a dog's chance of their getting back again without being smashed up against the ship's bows or against it's anchor as they and the Baltic pounded up and down. It was so sickening that I had to turn away at times*."

Unfortunately, Ortweiler also witnessed Rex Parson's last moments and the reaction of his distraught father who he described as:

> "...*like a man possessed, waving his arms in gestures of despair and looking over the side of the vessel. They say he made several attempts to cast off the line and leave himself to his fate. Eventually he seemed to hurl himself over the stern and tear himself along the line until he was hauled on board the lifeboat*."

Regrettably, Ortweiler's description of the men in the lifeboat is not borne out by examination of the *Baltic's* crew list. The youngest men were Peter Codd and George Delahay aged twenty-one years and the eldest was John Boylan aged fifty-three. There were a number of youngsters on board *Baltic* in their early teens, the youngest being John G. Scott aged fourteen years. They were all serving as page boys and none entered Lifeboat 10.

The New York Times ran their first account of the rescue on 7 December before the *Baltic* had arrived in New York, and a lengthier version on 11 December after they had had the opportunity to speak to those on board. The newspapers were not the only interested parties. In an interview some years later, Jim recounted that whilst ashore in New York he had been approached by an American advertising agent:

"I was offered 1000 dollars if I said I had smoked a certain brand of cigarette immediately after the rescue, but I refused."

Jim, a lifelong smoker who enjoyed a cigar, was clearly a man of enormous principles! At today's rate, he declined a little over $17,000 in exchange for a minor white lie.

Adding impetus to the story of the rescue was the revelation that one of the passengers on board the *Baltic* had taken a cine film of the rescue and its immediate aftermath. According to the story handed down through the Parsons family since 1929, the film-maker was a Cambridge University student. On arrival in New York on

10 December, the student made their way to the offices of Fox Movietone, where they sold their film for $125. Returning to the *Baltic*, Captain Tom Parsons was given the money by the student who was clearly moved by his plight and enormous loss. Fox developed the cine film into a news item that included a brief interview with Jim where his verbal account accompanies the flickering film. Jim briefly appears alongside an American presenter who is significantly taller that the 5ft 6inches tall Jim. This news film subsequently aired in movie theatres across the United States and United Kingdom as a precursor to the main feature film and Jim became something of a minor media celebrity. In the years after the rescue, it was not uncommon for him to go to theatres in towns where his ship had docked and give a short presentation about the rescue before the film was played and then have a short Q&A session with the audience. As a child in pre-war Liverpool, my late father recalled the film being shown at home on high days and holidays, and always at Christmas, projected onto a white sheet pinned to a wall. Fox syndicated the film and various silent and captioned versions of it were also produced; they can still be viewed today. Although I had met Jim once in 1964, I had no memory of his voice. It was quite a moment to hear him speak some ninety-three years after the rescue. I had always assumed he would have a distinct Liverpudlian accent but instead he had retained his easily identifiable, native, flat north-east, Hull lilt.

The *Baltic* arrived in New York on 10 December having battled against foul weather the whole way. The exhausted survivors of the *Northern Light* had spent most of the trip back in the sick bay simply resting. With the agreement of the British Consul in New York, Mr. Franklin authorised the *Baltic* to sail on to Halifax, Nova Scotia to get Parsons and his crew home. They were landed there on 16 December, bid a grateful farewell to Jim and his colleagues, and took a passage on the SS *Silvia*, finally arriving in St John's harbour on 19 December.

Captain Davies took the *Baltic* back across the Atlantic on an uneventful voyage, to everyone's relief, bringing her safely home into Liverpool on Christmas Eve 1929.

The new year and decade of 1930 saw Jim and his comrades from Lifeboat 10 being honoured on both sides of the Atlantic.

On 17 January, at Liverpool Town Hall, Captain Davies, Jim and six of the men from the lifeboat, were presented with gallantry awards. On behalf of the Liverpool Shipwreck and Humane Society, the Lord Mayor of Liverpool, Lawrence D. Holt, presented Davies with an illuminated address and silver medal. Jim received an illuminated address and a bar to his first Bramley-Moore medal (for the rescue of the *Daisy* in 1927) as well as a combined clock and barometer. Bramley-Moore medals and illuminated addresses went to Boylan, Fitzgerald, Whelan, Codd, Williams and Cole who also had attended that day.

On 21 February 1930, at the Gladstone Dock offices of the White Star Line, Captain Davies, Jim and the other nine men all received silver medals from the Corporation of Lloyds. Presented to them by Commodore Bartlett, he concluded the ceremony by saying,

"...you have already received well deserved recognition from other bodies, and it is now my privilege to hand to you all, on behalf of the great Corporation of Lloyds, the medals presented to you for your heroic conduct and I would like to tell you that the managers of the White Star Line, and all connected with the company, appreciate and are proud of what you have done on this occasion."

The Guildhall Library holds the original report submitted by Captain Davies, which includes accurate timings for the rescue with the *Northern Light* being sighted at 09:45am and rescuers and survivors back on board the *Baltic* and full speed ahead at 11:46am–the entire epic lasted two hours and one minute.

On 26 June, onboard the *Baltic* whilst she was moored again in New York, they were all awarded medals by the United States Life Saving Benevolent Association. Presented by Mr. Herbert Saterlee (brother-in-law of J.P. Morgan), Jim received a large gold medal and $100. His lifeboat crew received bronze medal pins and $100 each whilst Captain Davies also received a gold medal. Presenting Jim with his medal, Mr. Saterlee, the President of the Association said:

"I understand this is your second brave rescue. I am glad you have the habit. Keep it up."

In a brief address to his audience, Saterlee continued:

"Many a vessel has been wrecked and left to her

fate, but only because she had not been sighted. The Baltic not only sighted the Northern Light but by skillful manoeuvering in the hands of her Captain, lowered the boat in a violent sea and succeeded in accomplishing a gallant rescue."

On 14 March 1931, local papers reported that the Lord Mayor of Liverpool, Alderman Edwin Thompson, at the town hall, had presented Jim with a pair of binoculars on behalf of the Newfoundland Government in recognition, "of his services in assisting in the rescue".

Finally, on 26 June 1931, Jim and five of the other men from Lifeboat 10 went to Buckingham Palace and were decorated by George V with bronze Sea Gallantry Medals. Photographs taken that day show only Jim in uniform, the others all in suits and wearing smart hats. The weather that early summer day appears to have been perfect and the six men look to be thoroughly enjoying themselves. It was apparently the last investiture undertaken by George, who shortly afterwards became ill, retired to Sandringham and died five years later. By the end of 1931, Jim held five decorations for acts of gallantry at sea.

Captain Tom Parsons continued as a mariner on his return to Newfoundland, but he never again skippered a vessel, preferring to crew as a deckhand under his son Peter. He died in 1956. In September 2019, the Parsons family, keenly aware that young Rex Parsons has no grave and is not remembered anywhere, placed a simple stone plaque in the ground in front of his parent's grave in the cemetery at Musgravetown, Bonavista Bay, Newfoundland.

Chapter Eight

The collapse of the world economy and the onset of the Great Depression inevitably took its toll on the big shipping companies. White Star Line had been struggling financially for some years. Indeed, dwindling passenger numbers are perfectly illustrated by the fact that when the *Baltic* put to sea in November 1929 destined to enter maritime history books, she did so with only 326 passengers. She had a capacity to carry 2,800 passengers. They were significantly outnumbered in excess by the four hundred crew members required to run the ship. Indeed, E. P. Ortweiler's letter to his parents that was published in *The Times* on 23 December 1929 includes his reference to a collection amongst the passengers for the survivors that had raised £120: "A good sum for so small a passenger list."

Her main competitor, Cunard, was not faring much better, though they continued to push ahead and tried to expand their fleet. By 1933, both companies were in dire financial difficulties. Cunard approached the coalition, or national government of the day, presided over by Ramsey McDonald, and requested a loan to enable them to complete the construction of the *Queen Mary*. The government, keen to ensure that as many employees as possible in both organisations remained in jobs, would only loan the money to Cunard if they and the White Star line agreed to merge. Their concerns were valid; nearly thirteen million, 24.9% of the total workforce in the United Kingdom was currently unemployed. Whilst understandably reluctant, pragmatism won the day and on 10 May 1934 they merged, becoming Cunard White Star Line with Cunard owning 62% of the shares. Upon merger, the fleet comprised ten former White Star ships whilst Cunard contributed fifteen. Once the new company existed the government released £9.5 million to Cunard: £3 million for completion of the *Queen Mary*, £5 million to build the *Queen Elizabeth* and £1.5 million of working capital. In 1947, the year Jim would retire, Cunard bought the remaining 38% of shares from White Star's creditors and in 1949 completely dropped the name of White Star, simply using the name Cunard.

However, the name of White Star Line still lingers in the shadows, as today Cunard describes its high-end service as of 'White Star Standard'. Every 15 April, the Cunard fleet flies the iconic White Star flag as a tribute to the *Titanic* lost on that day in 1912. The nautical world has no truck with the petty tribal allegiances and jealousies that blight other industries. Cunard flies the White Star emblem not only to commemorate the *Titanic* but also to salute and acknowledge the marques integration and achievements.

Jim, and my grandfather Harry Owen, both transferred

into the Cunard family, but despite keeping their jobs, their careers stalled. The management of the Cunard White Star Line was wholly Cunard dominated and former White Star men were rarely, if ever, promoted into more senior appointments on Cunard ships. However, the reverse did happen. Cunard personnel were transferred onto former White Star ships and took senior positions regardless of their lack of qualifications and experience. For former White Star men, opportunities were few and far between and a case of dead men's shoes. A further source of concern was that the White Star Line had not had a pension fund and so as he neared the end of his career at sea, Jim's contributions into a pension for his retirement only commenced on the formation of Cunard White Star in 1934.

By his own extraordinary measure, the 1930s passed quietly for Jim, notwithstanding the growing menace from Nazi Germany. He spent most of 1930 and 1931 on the *Baltic*, criss-crossing the Atlantic between Liverpool and New York, usually as Third Mate. In the years that followed, he sailed on the *Georgic* regularly between Liverpool and Southampton to New York, Havana and Nassau. It was on these trips to sunnier climes that I suspect the photographs of Jim enjoying the company of dancing girls were taken. Voyages on *Aquitania*, *Andania*, *Berengaria* and *Franconia* followed before in 1939 he found himself back on an old White Star ship, the *Georgic*, sailing between Liverpool and New York. He was on board her in September 1939 when Britain declared war on Germany. His peace and quiet was shattered as the Cunard fleet moved under the control of the Royal Navy for the duration of the conflict. The year 1940 saw Jim on board the *Antonia* sailing between Liverpool and New York again, before on 3 May 1942 in Liverpool, he was engaged as the Senior First Officer on the *Laconia*. The description of the voyage in his discharge book is simply OHMS (On His Majesty's Service). It was a voyage that would end in catastrophe and of all the hundreds of trips Jim had made in his career and the incidents he had experienced, this was the one that had the most profound effect on him. He did not speak of it to the family subsequently and his only known reference to it is a single paragraph in the notes of his 1954 interview in which he describes it as, "the blackest spot of the war".

The *Laconia* sailed from Liverpool, in convoy, bound for Suez on 28 May 1942. Built in 1922 by Swan Hunter on the Tyne, the *Laconia* was 624 feet long and weighed nearly 20,000 tons. Twin-screwed, she was capable of reaching a top speed of seventeen knots. At the time of her launch as a Cunard passenger ship, she became the first passenger liner to circumnavigate the globe by gyro-compass during a winter cruise in 1922/23. She also boasted the world's largest floating laundry. A 1928 refit increased passenger accommodation to 347 first, 350 second and 1,500 third class. Passengers reported being hugely impressed by her luxury and comfort. A lounge had been built to resemble an English inn, with an inglenook fireplace and she also sported a ballroom, a library and her own printing office to print the on-board gossip magazine, *Cruising Topics*. Following the outbreak of war, she had undergone a significant conversion for troop carrying and convoy work and the ship that departed Liverpool in 1942 bore little internal resemblance to the masterpiece of twenty years earlier. She had not, however, lost her capability to make seventeen knots. This was intended to be Jim's second lengthy voyage on *Laconia* that year. On 7 January 1942, he had joined the ship for a four-month trip to the Middle East via Cape Hope and the Red Sea. That voyage had passed without incident and not surprisingly her captain, sixty-two-year old Rudolph Sharp had specifically requested that both Chief Officer George Sharp and Jim rejoin him on *Laconia's* next run south.

Also part of that convoy was the second incarnation of the *Britannic* with my grandfather, Harry Owen, on board. The convoy, escorted by the battleship *Nelson*, battle cruiser *Renown* and the Dutch cruiser *Heemskirk*, comprised a total of seventeen major ships. An uneventful voyage saw the convoy reach Port Tewfic on 26 July, where it disembarked some three thousand troops and many tons of equipment sent to reinforce the British Eighth Army in North Africa. The larger ships then returned to the United Kingdom the way they had come–via the Cape, but the *Laconia* remained in Port Tewfic to collect a very mixed bag of passengers for her return voyage. 1,793 Italian prisoners of war, captured by the Eighth Army, boarded and were placed in cages in the holds where they were to be guarded by Polish guards under the command of British Army officers. In addition to the Italian prisoners, some two hundred female prisoners were also brought on-board. Of various nationalities, they were accused of prostitution and fifth-column activities.

Over the next five weeks, the *Laconia* called at Aden, Mombasa, Durban and Cape Town and by the time she left there for the final leg of her voyage home, her passengers included 286 military personnel and eighty civilians–mainly women and children, the families of servicemen–a total, including the 463 crew, of 2,725. What *Laconia* did not have was lifeboat space for anything like that number; nor did she now have an escort. She was a sitting duck.

Laconia left Cape Town on 1 September and faced a seven thousand mile journey home alone. Captain Sharp plotted a zig-zag course by day, proceeding at full steam on a normal course under cover of darkness and kept *Laconia* well away from the coast to combat the threat of enemy aircraft; but they were still at real risk from a greater unseen threat–the German U-boat wolf packs.

The sinking of the Laconia – 12 September 1942
/// bassoonist.eyeful.unconditional

By 7:30pm on 12 September, *Laconia* was about nine hundred miles south of Freetown and 250 miles north-east of Ascension Island. As night had fallen, Captain Sharp had ordered the cessation of their zig-zag course and *Laconia* now steamed on a steady north-westerly course at around seventeen knots. She was being closely observed by Lt Cmdr Werner Hartenstein in U-156, one of more than three hundred submarines that Germany was able to keep at sea at any given time. Hartenstein was a regular officer, aged thirty-two years, university educated, who had joined the German Navy in 1928, before the

Nazi era, and had come through the ranks, transferring out of destroyers into the submarine corps. Unmarried, he was distinguished by a duelling scar on his left cheek. He was something of a celebrity in his hometown of Paluen in Saxony where U-156 had been adopted by the townspeople. In the eyes of his boss, Admiral Karl Donitz, head of the German U-boat fleet, Hartenstein was a man destined for high rank. He had been in command of U-156 since her launch in September 1941 and proved himself a very capable hunter. Between February and September of 1942, he had sunk twenty-two allied ships, totalling 105,232 tons, with significant loss of life. This was his fourth combat mission.

At just after 8:00pm, from about a mile away, Hartenstein dispatched U-156's first torpedo and at 8:07pm observed it tear into the starboard side of the *Laconia*, sealing the fate of the unfortunate Italian prisoners being held in Number 2 hold. Tons of water flooded into the huge hole and *Laconia* lurched violently to port, then rose and began listing to starboard only to be flung again from side to side as thirty seconds later a second torpedo smashed through the hull into the engine room. Few survived in the engine room; everyone in the firemen's quarters perished in their cabins. The lights failed, making it more difficult too for passengers and crew to find their way to their boat stations. In the confusion, children became separated from their mothers. Several of the ship's already inadequate supply of lifeboats were destroyed by the blasts. Captain Sharp realised immediately that his ship was mortally wounded and issued the order to 'abandon ship', an order conveyed around the ship by word of mouth as all the telephones had been put out of action. Chief Officer Steel and Jim were dispatched from the bridge to the boat deck to supervise the launching of what lifeboats they had whilst Sharp watched on from his bridge.

Unsurprisingly, chaos ensued. Within minutes of the ship being hit, many of the Italian prisoners being held below managed to force their way out of their cages and began to try and make their way up to the boat deck and escape. The British officer in charge of the Polish guards, Lt Col Baldwin, took extreme measures to calm the situation and prevent the Italians from overwhelming the few boats. Assisted by Capt McCordick and Lt Dickens (Royal Artillery), together with some of the Polish guards, Baldwin took up a position at the top of the main staircase leading up from the hold and fired a hail of bullets into the crowd coming up from below. In the darkness it was impossible to distinguish who was actually in the panicking mob and surviving *Laconia* crew members later recounted that some of the *Laconia's* own catering crew had likely been shot dead by mistake. Some desperate Italian prisoners who did make it up onto the boat deck began to fight the passengers and amongst themselves, for a place in one of the lifeboats and a number were bayonetted by the Polish guards who had not been issued with ammunition. Working feverishly amidst the mayhem, the crew of the *Laconia* began to start getting their lifeboats away. They were largely filled with women and children, the first of which crashed against the side of the ship and capsized, tipping its occupants into the water. Panic and confusion spread on the boat deck as it became clear there were far too few lifeboats on the ship and then to compound the horror, those struggling in the sea became aware of a greater terror – sharks.

As passengers began to succumb to the shark attacks and their blood drained into the sea, the sharks increased in numbers and began to attack anything moving. Some of the Italian prisoners had jumped into the sea and swam towards the lifeboats and were now threatening to capsize them as they desperately tried to haul themselves aboard and escape the circling sharks. On Lifeboat 17, the ship's plumber, Charles Gregory, was handed an axe and instructed to chop off the fingers of the Italians trying to get on board. Reluctant to do so, he demurred until a Royal Navy rating who was busily slicing off hands and fingers shouted at him to take action against an Italian who had hauled himself half-way into the boat, threatening to tip all the occupants into the lethal sea. Gregory hit the man on the head with the flat end of the axe and, full of guilt and remorse, watched the corpse float away into the darkness. Now, those fortunate to have got into a lifeboat had to endure blood-chilling screams from out in the darkness as the sharks attacked the living and the dead in the water. Jim had taken charge of one of the lifeboats and now began to get as many survivors as possible, both British passengers and Italian prisoners, into his lifeboat.

Captain Sharp and Chief Officer Steel had chosen to remain on the *Laconia* and had gone onto the bridge. Survivors in the lifeboats alongside the ship saw the glow of two cigarettes from the bridge and then at 9:20pm the stern of the ship lifted high out of the water and with a roar from the funnel, the *Laconia* slid down into the sea taking men, women and children with her.

Shortly before she had gone down, Hartenstein brought U-156 towards *Laconia* with the aim of implementing Admiral Donitz's instructions to his captains, to take captive wherever possible, the captain and engineer of ships they had sunk. This eminently sensible instruction was intended to deprive the British Merchant service of its most experienced officers. Initially concerned that the stern gun on the *Laconia* might open fire on his vessel, he relaxed until he realised that in the lifeboats and swimming among the debris on the sea's surface were women and children and that he could hear Italian as well as English voices. The full horror of what had happened rapidly became apparent to him. U-156 began to approach the lifeboats and a German officer asked each boat in perfect English if any officers were on board. Jim was well aware of the German's intentions and warned those sitting in his boat to reply 'no'.

Hartenstein began to recover survivors from the wreckage-strewn water. He was well aware that unless rescue came soon, many of those in the boats and certainly, those in the water, would not survive long. Accordingly, he ordered a signal to be sent to Admiral Donitz back in the headquarters of U-boat command on the Avenue Marechal Maunoury in Paris:

> *"British liner Laconia sunk by Hartenstein. Ship unfortunately carrying 1500 Italian prisoners of war. So far 90 rescued. Request instructions."*

Donitz ordered him to remain where he was but to be ready to submerge. Early on Sunday 13 September, Hartenstein transmitted another message, in English, on the twenty-five metre band:

> *"If any ship will assist the shipwrecked Laconia crew*
> *I will not attack her provided I am not attacked by*
> *ship or air forces. I picked up 193 men 4* 52' south,*
> *11* 26' west. German submarine."*

Ten minutes later he repeated the message on the six-hundred metre international wavelength. Back in Paris, Donitz decided to support Hartenstein in his humanitarian efforts and ordered two of his submarines operating off Cape Town, U-506 and U-507, to break off their operations and proceed at full speed to assist Hartenstein. Reportedly, Adolf Hitler was furious when informed of the decision, but it was not countermanded. Admiral Raeder, Naval Commander-in-Chief, then successfully set in motion an approach to the Vichy French government and persuaded them to use their naval vessels located in North Africa to assume responsibility for the rescue.

As dawn broke, using a loud hailer, Hartenstein called out to the occupants of the lifeboats to come alongside U-156. Initially very reluctant to do so, their reserve disappeared when they saw that the German captain was providing hot coffee and soup. Eight of the lifeboats came alongside and several were taken in tow. A further two-hundred or so survivors, including 150 Italians were taken onto the deck of U-156. Four British women were taken below, their clothing dried and they were given bunks to rest in. Hartenstein and his crew appeared to be genuinely moved by the condition of their civilian victims and one, Doris Hawkins, recalled later:

> *"The Germans treated us with kindness and respect the whole time, they were really sorry for our plight. One brought us eau de cologne, another cold cream for our sunburn which was really bad, others gave us lemons from their lockers, articles of clothing and tinned fruit. The commandant (sic) was particularly charming and helpful."*

The Vichy French dispatched the sloops *Dumont-d'Urville* and *Annamite* together with the large cruiser *Gloire* from their berths in the West African port of Dakar. They were instructed to rendezvous with the German U-boats they would find in situ and take off survivors from them. However, the rescuers all had considerable distances to travel; rescue would not be coming soon.

By 13 September, those in charge of the lifeboats had been obliged to institute rigid rationing of water and food. Discipline among the Italians was poor and in his lifeboat, Jim had to take action against eight of them who he suspected had drained three of the four water tanks. He made an example of them by forcing them to fill the bare space left by the tanks and nailing planks of wood across to keep them confined. Conditions on the lifeboats quickly became dire. Overcrowded and cramped, it was impossible for anyone to lie down. Frequently room had to be made to allow bailing. The men nearest the sides of the boats were afforded the opportunity to sit on the gunwales, but could easily fall overboard if they fell asleep. Towards midnight that day, those in charge of four of the boats that had managed to stay close to each other, began to consider what to do next. Either set sail westwards towards the South American coast or north-eastwards towards the African coast. Brazil was nearly one thousand miles away, the African coast slightly closer at six hundred miles and they had more hope of being spotted if an air search from British bases in Africa was underway. They agreed a plan; at 9:00am the following day, 14 September, they would hoist sails and commence their long journey towards the African coast. Each boat was to follow in line, keeping the sail of the boat ahead just in sight. Their simple plan gave the boats a range of fifteen miles visibility north-east and south-west and three miles on each side of that line. They hoped that in a few days they should arrive in the southern fringes of the Doldrums where they could expect violent thunderstorms and torrential rainfall, unpleasant but vital to replenish their dwindling supply of water.

Lt Col Baldwin on board one of the lifeboats, became concerned with the mental deterioration of two of the *Laconia's* crew on board; Chief Purser Tom Cullum who went raving mad and had to be restrained, and Storekeeper Jack Moore who had been drinking sea water, a short-cut to madness. Baldwin considered them both a threat to them all. His concerns were shared by Cpt Atkins, Royal Artillery, who took a dim view of the *Laconia's* crew. With a few exceptions, he thought them a poor lot and their officers too old. Captain Sharp was fifty-six, Chief Officer Steel fifty-eight and Jim fifty-five; they were certainly not in the first flush of youth. The youngest officer to survive the sinking was Junior Third Officer Ellis who was twenty-one. Atkins also thought it incomprehensible that an old ship was allowed to proceed unescorted at the mercy of U-boats, and criminal to place women and children on a ship transporting prisoners of war. Baldwin and Atkins agreed a pending action to dispose of Cullum and Moore overboard to safeguard the welfare of the majority. Thankfully, both men were rescued by the Vichy French before Baldwin and Atkins put their plan into effect.

At 7:30am on 14 September, Donitz ordered his U-boats engaging in the rescue to accept:

"...only such numbers (of survivors) as will ensure the boat still remains operational when submerged."

This troubled Hartenstein as he now had over two hundred survivors in or on U-156. He was well aware that to submerge would be to abandon those on the deck to their fate. On 15 September U-506, under Lt Cmdr Wuerdemann, arrived in the area and Hartenstein transferred 130 Italians to U-506, keeping fifty-five Italians and fifty-five British on his submarine. Wuerdemann then returned to the actual site of the sinking in the hope of meeting up with the French warships that he knew had been dispatched, or the Italian submarine *Cappellini* which was in the area. That afternoon, U-507 under Lt

Cmdr Schacht arrived and began to collect survivors from lifeboats that had drifted away from the sinking site. In total, the U-boats pulled together eight lifeboats, including the small flotilla heading for the African coast. Schacht took all eight in tow with instructions that a man armed with an axe should be positioned forward in each boat to cut the tow rope in the event of an attack by aircraft. Some distance away, Hartenstein had another four lifeboats under tow.

Chapter Nine

For some months, and in great secrecy, the Americans had been building an airfield on Ascension Island with the aim of providing air support to allied shipping in the South Atlantic. By September 1942, the United States Air Force 1ˢᵗ Composite Squadron had begun flying sorties over the area the *Laconia* had been sunk.

Admiral Donitz and his U-boat fleet were completely oblivious to the presence of the airfield. It appears that neither the Americans on Ascension Island nor the British in Freetown had picked up Hartenstein's messages about the sinking. More strangely, the British who had cracked the German's Enigma codes and were capable of reading all the communications between the Nazi military command, had apparently intercepted nothing.

On 16 September, the Americans dispatched a B24 Liberator bomber piloted by Lt James Harden, in response to a belated request from the British to provide some air cover for two ships now engaged in the search for survivors from the missing *Laconia*. By 9:30am he was flying above U-156, now towing four lifeboats and with numerous survivors on the deck. Hartenstein had raised a home-made Red Cross flag and tried unsuccessfully to make contact with the aircraft by way of morse light signals sent from the deck by a British Wing Commander. The RAF officer's morse signal could not have been clearer:

"RAF officer speaking from German submarine, Laconia survivors on board, soldiers, civilians, women, children..."

Harden, who later said he tried to get the submarine to disclose its nationality, signalled his base back on Ascension for instructions. He made no mention of the presence of the lifeboats under tow, or the flying of the Red Cross flag (though he referred to them in his final report), and significantly he later admitted he could not read the morse signals from the submarine's deck. Having told his base he was sure the submarine was German, he was ordered to attack it. The Liberator made four runs altogether, dropping several bombs and depth charges. One fell among the lifeboats as they were being cast off, capsizing one and causing numerous deaths. Several fell alongside U-156 and Hartenstein, his submarine quite badly damaged, was forced to submerge, leaving the survivors on deck, mostly Italian prisoners, to fend for themselves. Many were dragged down with the submarine.

A few miles away, Schacht and Wuerdemann were furious to hear of the attack on their colleague, yet they continued to shepherd their survivors, remaining on the surface, ever vigilant. On 17 September, having returned to the surface and once again towing lifeboats he had managed to recover, Hartenstein was informed in a radio message that he had been awarded the Knights Cross of the Iron Cross for his actions in undertaking the rescue.

At 10:30am on 18 September, Lt Harden and his crew returned again, and now attacked U-506 and U-507 with bombs and depth charges. Both submarines submerged, dooming the poor souls on deck and only Wuerdemann's ploy of sending an oil slick to the surface persuaded Harden that he had destroyed at least one of the submarines and he broke off the attack. He returned to Ascension Island for tea and medals.

Soon after, the French vessels *Gloire*, *Annamite* and *Dumont d'Urville* arrived along with the Italian submarine *Cappellini*. A total of 650 survivors were transferred to the French ships, the British among them destined for internment in Vichy French camps near Casablanca. Jim was taken on board the *Gloire* which now headed for Dakar, arriving there on 22 September, where she refuelled and provisioned before commencing the last leg of the journey to Casablanca, where they arrived on 24 September. The British Admiralty received a secret cypher on 1 October which gave some detail of the British survivors, now prisoners, arrival at Casablanca:

"Members of crew of Gloire stated impressed by the model behaviour of British sailors picked up, whereas Italians were simply insufferable, insolent and arrogant. On landing at Casablanca, the Italians had priority and went off first, without a

word of thanks. The British however, before setting off in the lorries lined up along the quay, gave three cheers for the Captain and crew of the Gloire and shouted 'Vive la France'. Those of the ship's company who were previously pro-collaboration have now definitely changed their tune."

It appears that it was the brutish Lt Col Baldwin who led the British in their salute to the French crew. The propaganda war never sleeps.

Not all the lifeboats that had got away from the *Laconia* had been found by the U-boats or the French vessels. One came ashore in Liberia, West Africa, on 9 October. Of the original sixty-four occupants, only sixteen had survived. Another, one that had become isolated and drifted away after the first American attack, was not located until 21 October, ironically Trafalgar Day, and recovered by the British ship HMS *Wiston*.

After six days in an open lifeboat, Jim was finally back on dry land, and with the rest of the male British prisoners he was transported to Mediouna Camp, twenty kilometres along the Marrakesh road. The women and children were separated from the men and taken to another camp nearby.

The scale of the tragedy that had engulfed those on the *Laconia* became apparent to the British soon after the prisoners had been landed at Casablanca. On 27 September, Prime Minister Winston Churchill sent a memo to the First Sea Lord:

"The report of 650 survivors being brought in from the Laconia and another ship, shows that a very serious tragedy has taken place. Is it known what proportion are British personnel? There were nearly 3000 people to be accounted for, so over 2000 must have lost their lives."

Churchill's figures were almost right. Whilst figures vary slightly, it appears that 450 Italian prisoners survived from the nearly 1,800 on board, 588 of the 829 British (crew and passengers) and 73 of the 103 Polish guards. The death toll was in the region of 1,621. Such a loss would require an official investigation. There was clearly a blame game developing and early in October, the American ambassador in Casablanca interviewed some of the survivors, civilian and military, and put together a report that was sent to the British government:

"A sorry story with some useful suggestions:

My personal experience of passage in a transport (without prisoners), an experience shared by many with whom I have yarned, is that the Merchant Navy is very reluctant to take any measures that savour of discipline.

The question of who should take charge of boats crops up frequently but I think personality decides.

The U-boat did not track Laconia and it is extremely unlikely that they knew her route, but

they very likely knew of her passage from the Cape.
It is evident from other sources that her smoke was
seen at a great distance, and one report states that
she made a large arc towards the U-boat when she
was rapidly going out of sight."

On 22 December, the homicidal Lt Col Baldwin, officer in charge of the Italian prisoners and their Polish guards, with a Wing Commander Blackburn, went to the War Office in London to lodge an official complaint about the inefficiency of the *Laconia's* crew and the poor condition of the lifeboats. Squadron Leader Vincent Mears supported their complaint by stating that the *Laconia's* rafts were tied together with rope, fastened to the bulkheads, and not one member of the crew was assigned the responsibility to release them in time of emergency. He also criticised the boat drills.

The Board of Trade duly convened a preliminary enquiry into the circumstances surrounding the *Laconia's* sinking and on 15 February 1943 it issued a statement:

"Suggestions lifeboats leaked and not provisioned
properly mainly hearsay. Depositions taken by the
Receiver of Wrecks from six members of the crew,
including three senior officers, each of whom pays high
tribute to the behaviour of the crew. Taking all the
circumstances into consideration and account, it is not
considered any good purpose will be served by a more
formal inquiry, nor does the further evidence indicate
that disciplinary action would be justified as regards

*the Merchant Navy crew. The experience gained will
be used to the best advantage for the future."*

It is a statement straight out of today's National Health
Service playbook, where one health trust after another
promises to 'learn lessons' having presided over yet
another scandalous loss of life. It is very likely that one
of the three senior officers interviewed by the Receiver of
Wrecks was Jim. Of the eight officers on the bridge of the
Laconia, only four survived and as Senior First Officer, Jim
was the most senior of the surviving officers.

Frederick Grossmith, in his seminal work, *"The
Sinking of the Laconia"*, on which I have drawn extensively,
describes this quite blatant cover-up perfectly:

*"That act of officialdom closed the book on the
Laconia epic, not daring to draw attention to the grave
matter of the Italian prisoners of war. Of the persons
who survived from the Laconia approximately 450
were Italians. Hartenstein's torpedoes, the sea and
the American bomber accounted for the majority
of their deaths, but many met death under a hail of
bullets when they tried to reach the upper decks after
escaping from their prison hatch; a matter not spoken
about, save in hushed tones by certain crew members.
No one even seems to have raised the question as to
how, thirty years after the scandalous tragedy of the
Titanic, a ship could have sailed the Atlantic with
an insufficient number of lifeboats to accommodate
everyone on board."*

That was not the end of repercussions from the sinking. After the American attacks on his submarines attempting to rescue the survivors of the *Laconia*, an infuriated Admiral Donitz interpreted them as evidence that the allies were prepared to sacrifice women and children to gain any advantage. On 17 September 1942 he issued an order titled 'Triton Null', better known as The Laconia Order:

> *"No attempts of any kind must be made to rescue members of ships sunk and this includes picking up persons in the water, putting them in lifeboats, righting capsized lifeboats and handing over food and water. Rescue runs counter to the most primitive demands of warfare for the destruction of enemy ships and crews."*

His order finished with the rather petulant instruction:

> *"Be hard. Remember the enemy has no regard for women and children when he bombs German cities."*

Donitz conveniently chose to overlook the huge air attacks suffered by British cities since 1940. In Liverpool alone, *Laconia's* home port, sixty-eight attacks between 1940 and 1941 had killed 3,966 of its citizens, injured as many, destroyed 6,500 homes and badly damaged 125,000 others. Parts of the East End of London had been flattened and thousands killed and injured. The suffering of German women and children would not have generated much empathy in Britain.

Following the death of Adolf Hitler, Donitz was informed by Martin Borman that the Fuhrer had designated him as his successor as Reich President. He ruled the disintegrating Reich for twenty days before he accepted the allied surrender terms on 8 May 1945. He was arrested on 22 May and charged with a number of war crimes, including one relating to his Laconia Order.

The quote "history is written by the victors" is often attributed to Winston Churchill, and it would unquestionably have been applied to Admiral Donitz's reputation save for some poor judgement by the Americans. The introduction of the Laconia Order into evidence against Donitz backfired spectacularly against the Americans as the Defence Counsel was able to call witnesses and it became clear how events had actually unfolded. Forced into a humiliating apology, the Americans reluctantly provided the tribunal with written testimony from Fleet Admiral Chester Nimitz, their wartime Commander-in-Chief of the United States Pacific fleet, on behalf of Donitz's defence, unapologetically admitting that the United States had been waging unrestricted submarine warfare since their entry into the war using their own version of a Laconia Order. Whilst the tribunal in its judgement agreed that the evidence did not show that he had ordered the deliberate killing of shipwrecked survivors, his orders were undoubtedly ambiguous and deserved the strongest censure. Found guilty of the other crimes and sentenced to ten years imprisonment, he was quite rightly acquitted of the charge relating to that order.

Importantly, there is no evidence that U-boat commanders ever implemented the Laconia Order; indeed, *there is* evidence that some deliberately ignored it, swore their crews to secrecy, and assisted shipwrecked survivors. There was a school of thought at the time that the only war crimes committed during the *Laconia* incident were allied. Many felt that it was simply incomprehensible that Lt Harden had not seen the lifeboats under tow behind the U-boats or the survivors on the open decks and that the instruction of his commander on Ascension Island and his attacks on the U-boats constituted a war crime.

Donitz died on Christmas Eve 1980 and was buried near Hamburg. There were no military honours or government representatives but five-thousand Kreigsmarine veterans attended to pay their last respects.

None of his U-boat crews involved in the sinking of the *Laconia* and the subsequent rescue attempts survived the war; Hartenstein and his crew were killed in action east of Barbados on 8 March 1943, Schacht and his crew earlier on 13 January 1943, and Wuerdemann and his men on 14 July 1943. All were killed as a result of attacks by American aircraft.

Lt Harden and his Liberator bomber crew were awarded Air Medals for the destruction of an enemy submarine on 16 September 1942 and the probable destruction of another on 17 September. As a work of fiction, the citation takes some beating. They all survived the war.

Chapter Ten

Jim was not incarcerated for long. 1942 had been a dreadful year, an appalling succession of disasters for the Allies; the fall of Singapore in February, the greatest military capitulation in British military history was simply the worst of many setbacks that year. The loss of so many lives aboard the *Laconia* seemed to finish the year off perfectly. Desperate for some good news to stimulate an increasingly war-weary public, on 8 November 1942 the Allies launched Operation Torch, landing troops in North Africa. By 10 November the town of Oran had surrendered and the Allies firmly entrenched. The prisoners in Medioura Camp and elsewhere were liberated by American troops and Jim soon returned to Britain, via Norfolk, Virginia.

After a period of recuperation and minor surgery for a stomach ailment, at the venerable age of fifty-six, Jim married Florence (Florrie) Owen, my grandfather's half-sister, on 19 December 1942 in Crosby Register Officer. Jim's profession was given as Master Mariner, Merchant Marine, whilst Florrie merited a line through the box.

She was recorded as a thirty-seven year old spinster whilst there is a detailed entry for Jim who it noted was "formerly the husband of Mary Putt Walker formerly Rouse (sic), spinster, from whom he obtained a divorce". The witnesses to their marriage were Florrie's elder sister Mabel and her brother-in-law Joseph Hughes and the happy couple gave their address as 31 Coronation Drive, Crosby. His best friend Harry Owen would undoubtedly have been present had he not been at sea. Interestingly, it appears that Florrie had been using the surname Walker for some time. In the 1939 census, she is recorded living at 54 Trinity Road, Bootle, with her elder sisters Mabel and Elsie and her brother-in-law Joseph Hughes, using the name Florence Walker. Jim and Florrie had known each other for years through Jim's friendship with Harry and she would without doubt have been aware of what Jim had endured during his years at sea. From a seafaring family, she would make the ideal companion for a mariner.

Alas, there is a very strong possibility that the marriage was bigamous. There is no trace of a Divorce Absolute of Jim's 1915 marriage in the records of the Family Court and when Mary Putt Walker made her will in 1948, six years after his marriage to Florrie, she did so in the very firm belief that she was still married to Jim. Her will specifically excludes Jim from any inheritance on the grounds that she had not seen, or heard from him in many years, they had only lived together very briefly having married, and Jim had not supported or maintained her in any way. Her estate was left to her elder brother Charles and her sisters Louie and Emmie. I had only become aware of his first marriage very recently and felt that it smacked of the 'shotgun' variety, particularly due to the significant members of her family who had not attended it. However, I have not found any evidence of a child born to the couple, Mary makes no bequest to a child in her will and her death in 1949 was reported by her sister Louie.

Frederick Grossmith concludes his wonderful account of the *Laconia* sinking with a story that I cannot help but think is about Jim. Each year on the anniversary of the sinking, bereaved families of crew members received a letter from a writer who signed himself as 'a *Laconia* survivor'. In 1967 the letters stopped and the identity of this crewman was never known. That last letter one of the recipients received in September 1966 was, as always, accompanied by a £1 note and contained some words of comfort. Doris Maddocks, daughter of Steward John Banks who had been lost, was sent the sentence:

"The beautiful music and rendering of Psalm 130 during this morning's 10.15am BBC Daily Service was so fitting for thoughts in my mind, and too, because of yesterday's anniversary of a day now so long passed."

Psalm 130–King James version
Out of the depths have I cried unto thee, O Lord
Lord hear my voice, let thine ears be attentive to the
*   voice of my supplications*
If thou, Lord, shouldest mark iniquities, O Lord who
*   shall stand?*
But there is forgiveness with thee, that thou mayest be
*   feared*

*I wait for the Lord, my soul doth wait and in his word
    do I hope*
*My soul waiteth for the Lord more than they that
    watch for the morning: I say, more than they that
    watch for the morning*
*Let Israel hope in the Lord: for with the Lord there is
    mercy, and with him is plenteous redemption*
And he shall redeem Israel from all his iniquities

One interpretation of the Psalm is that it is a personal testimony of rescue by God from the depths of guilt, a prayer for pardon and mercy. For someone haunted by what had happened on the *Laconia*, it clearly offers some comfort. If indeed Jim was the annual writer of those letters, I feel sure this Psalm would have helped him deal with the horror he had witnessed and perhaps felt responsible for in some way.

Jim died in December 1966, two months after the last of the letters arrived, in Liverpool, aged eighty; he was a regular churchgoer all his life.

Jim was back at sea in January 1943 as Chief Officer on the *Samaria*. His engagement and discharge book makes for interesting reading. During wartime, merchant seamen had the curious status of unarmed civilians plying their trade on the frontline. As civilians, they were paid danger money (initially £5 a week, later £10) while on 'articles', i.e., actually at sea. But when a ship was sunk, the articles were deemed to be closed, so the danger money stopped. Merchant seamen were not paid danger money for sitting in open lifeboats or clinging to rafts in freezing or shark-infested water. Jim's engagement on the *Laconia's* final voyage shows the place of engagement as Liverpool on 3 May 1942, his place of discharge on 12 September 1942 is shown as, 'at sea'.

Jim's first voyage after the sinking, on the *Samaria*, merited an entry–"Renewal book issued free of charge. Original reported lost through enemy action". The generosity of the Admiralty knew no bounds. My uncle, Robert (Bob) Owen, experienced similar treatment during the war. Twice forced into open lifeboats after a sinking, his danger money was stopped and on being rescued, required to purchase his own new clothes. On one occasion when he was brought into a Scottish port having been torpedoed off Reykjavik and suffering from frostbite in both feet, whilst service personnel were immediately disembarked, the merchant seamen had to go through Customs, where they were asked if they had anything to declare. I like to think that Bob responded appropriately.

Early in 1945, Jim finally took command of his own ship, the *Simcoe Park*. He spent some time in Vancouver watching her construction and his first voyage on her was back to Liverpool where he was when the German surrender was declared in May. In November 1946 he took command of the SS *Samouse*, a liberty ship delivered to Britain under Lend-Lease terms and in March 1947 he arrived with his vessel in Los Angeles. On 20 March he reported back to Cunard White Star that his ship had been boarded and searched by United States Customs officers on arrival earlier in Seattle on 11 and 12 March. The Customs officers had found various unmanifested goods concealed around the ship which Jim listed for his employers. The stash found by the searchers included twelve cases of whisky, eighteen bottles of rum, 600 pairs of ladies Rayon hosiery and 150 pairs of gents red woollen socks. Back in bleak, rationed Britain, these items would have been veritable gold dust. All the items were removed from the ship by the Customs officers who informed Jim that they would provide him with a full report, but by 15 March when he sailed, he had heard nothing. It is probably fair to assume that the seized goods had gone back into the black market.

Jim did, however, conduct his own enquiries, questioning a Greaser whose cabin had been found to be concealing the gents socks; he claimed they had been given to him by a labourer when the ship had called at Punta Cordon, Venezuela, in January. An even more unlikely explanation came from the Fourth Engineer, in whose cabin two dozen pairs of stockings had been found. These, he explained, he had found concealed in the engine room some time earlier and he had taken them to his cabin for safe keeping–but had neglected to tell anyone about his find.

Life at sea for lengthy periods had taken its toll on Jim; he had had enough and decided what he really wanted was to see out his remaining years with his beloved Florrie. Aged sixty-one, he retired from Cunard White Star in April 1947, after forty-six years at sea. He returned to the house he had bought on 19 August 1945 for the mortgage free sum of £1,775 at 6 Coronation Drive, Crosby, and threw himself into the life of an active retired person.

He hadn't moved far, literally just down the road from number 31. Number 6, named 'Garth', was, and still is, a handsome, solidly built, red-brick Edwardian semi-detached house, built in 1904 and just a few short steps from Alexandra Park where he began to walk regularly. He became a keen gardener, decorated the house from top to bottom, attended church regularly, became active in his local Freemason's Lodge, canvassed on behalf of the local Conservative Party, and took on a role with the Sea Cadets. In 1950, his brother-in-law, Joseph Hughes, died, and Mabel, Florrie's elder sister and her two sons Robert and Trevor moved in with them at 6 Coronation Drive. His time alone with Florrie had been brief, but it appears that he was agreeable to the arrangement. As a hobby, he began to build miniature ships in bottles, largely depicting the ships he had served on. As far as I am aware, only one of those models has survived–the one he gave me in 1964, of the *Santon*. In the early 1960s, Jim acquired a pet, a white French poodle that he called Tina, who became a constant companion on his walks around Alexandra Park; he appears to have adapted to civilian life easily.

On 11 December 1966, having suffered from type 2 diabetes for some years, Jim suffered a massive heart attack and died at home. He was cremated at Thornton Gardens Crematorium on 15 December and his ashes later scattered in the Garden of Remembrance. The service of committal was attended by a small number of friends and family who sang just one hymn as he was committed–'Eternal Father Strong to Save'.

His passing appears to have gone largely unmarked

in both his city of birth and adopted city. A small death notice in the *Liverpool Echo*, placed by the family, is the only acknowledgement I can find. It is odd and sad that the death of a man who represented two cities, particularly Liverpool, so courageously and became something of a celebrity in the 1930s, should have generated absolutely no interest.

Jim does not have a gravestone or other memorial, but he is remembered by our family on significant dates with the flying of a White Star Line flag at my home. I hope to persuade Liverpool City Council that he deserves a Blue Plaque somewhere significant to him in Liverpool. I hope this account of his remarkable life will help bring that about.

Chapter Eleven

Jim was a child of the Victorian age of Empire, born into the teeming back streets of Hull in conditions that Charles Dickens would have recognised and despaired of. Like so many of his generation, he was destined to serve through two World Wars and to endure unspeakable hardship. He may well have been able to sit out World War II because of his age, but typically he chose to serve. He was a seaman in the greatest mercantile fleet to ever sail the world's oceans, an absolute necessity in order to service the needs of an empire that, at its height, included nearly a quarter of the world's land mass and controlled 23% of its population.

His generation, in their tens of thousands, left the shores of this tiny island and went to the four corners of the earth, planting the British flag and thereafter nurturing and protecting the Empire they had created with their immense sea power, both militarily and economically. I make no comment on the rights and wrongs of the Empire, but just point out that Jim was a small cog in a machine that created and ran the largest empire since the Romans. He was a part of it at its absolute peak in the

1920s and a witness to its decline and fall in the aftermath of World War II as Britain's global influence significantly diminished and its colonies went their own ways.

He went to sea as a child of fifteen under sail, was shipwrecked twice, decorated for gallantry at sea five times, circumnavigated the globe endlessly and saw in the age of steam power at sea. His service with the iconic White Star Line coincided perfectly with the peak of its considerable power and influence and its decline and eventual disappearance.

On the face of it, Jim's personal life was complicated. Other than his 1915 marriage when his father and elder brother attended, there is absolutely no evidence that he retained any contact with his family thereafter. Virtually nothing is known of that first marriage in Hull, other than what can be gleaned from the marriage certificate and Mary's 1948 will. Almost certainly, Jim did not divorce Mary before his marriage in 1942 to Florrie in Liverpool. There is no evidence of children from his first marriage and there were none from his second, and questions about the first marriage remain unanswered. Clearly, he abandoned Mary very soon after their marriage, but why? In the years following his marriage he chose to spend extended periods at sea. Had his second voyage in 1942 on *Laconia* not been curtailed by Hartenstein's torpedoes, he would have been at sea that year for over nine months. Again, why? Are there direct descendants of his scattered around the globe? Imaginations can run riot.

Living memories of Jim are few and faint. Only my

cousin Jennifer has anything like a clear recollection of him and her memories are those of a seven or eight year old. She simply recalls that parties at his house or those that he attended at hers, were lively and full of laughter. My memory of my sole meeting with him in 1964 is simply that he was a small and stocky man with dark hair brushed back and glasses. I do not recall his wife, my great-aunt Florrie, or his dog Tina, being present. Of the house at 6 Coronation Drive, I can only remember that there was a lamp on the post at the bottom of the bannisters that had a Tiffany-style lampshade and there was stained glass in a window at the front of the house. The lamp is no longer there but the current owners tell me that when they bought the house in 1994, holes in the post indicated that something had once been secured there. And of course, he gave me a ship in a bottle. I don't remember him asking me to choose a bottle or simply handing one to me, but my parents told me years later that he had given it to me. It has been treasured ever since and has survived numerous postings to Army bases in the Far East, Germany and around the United Kingdom.

Jim was probably typical of his generation, with a keen sense of duty, of who he was and where he came from. We are fortunate that a description of him aged forty-six in 1932 exists to give a snapshot of the man. On board the *Themistocles*, en route from Australia to the United Kingdom, the ship had docked in Durban and Jim had been interviewed at some length about his famous sea rescues. The interviewing journalist was clearly very taken by him:

"These medals are for saving the crew of a French schooner and those for the rescue of five members of an abandoned Canadian fishing schooner," said Second Officer J Holland Walker (sic) of the White Star Liner Themistocles in port this morning from Australia, showing me a box of medals for lifesaving. I had to persuade him to do so, for not only in appearance but in modesty was he a typical sailor–quiet but as firm as a rock. A strong jaw but a boyish, pleasant face; 46 years of age yet looking not a day more than 35. Short and powerfully built with massive arms, useful I thought, in scrambling aboard a ship from a lifeboat. "He's probably saved more lives than any other officer in the Mercantile Marine", said a sailor who told me about Mr Walker."

Remarkable things occurred around him that he embraced, and whilst in the grand telling of the history of British maritime events his role was small, it is immensely rewarding to be able all these years after his passing, to tell his descendants of his place in them.

James Holland Walker

Born 1 April 1886 in Hull, died 11 December 1966 in
Liverpool

A White Star Line hero.

Service Medals and Sea Gallantry Awards

World War 1
British War Medal
Mercantile Marine Medal
Victory Medal

World War 2
1939–1945 Star
Atlantic Star
Africa Star
Clasp to Africa Star
Pacific Star
War Medal

Sea Gallantry Medals
Bronze Sea Gallantry Medal
Liverpool Shipwreck and Humane Society Bramley-
Moore Medal
Bar to Bramley-Moore Medal
Lloyds Medal for Saving Life at Sea
Medal of Honour, Marine Marchande

Chapter Twelve

The remarkable cine film of 6 December 1929 must be among the earliest of a rescue at sea ever taken. I had never thought beyond that until my friend Dave Burge casually remarked, 'I wonder which of the passengers took the film?', and we were off down that particular rabbit hole (one of many whilst researching this book).

We agreed that the easiest and most obvious way to find out would be to ask Fox Movietone Archives if they had the original receipt of sale but, having initially been very helpful, they stopped answering my emails! We then decided that the passenger list would provide some clues and working on several not unreasonable assumptions, we eventually secured a passenger list and began to go through it. Because of the story passed down through the Parsons family, we assumed that:

- The film maker was male,
- He was a Cambridge University student,
- He was probably a United States citizen returning home for Christmas,

- He was either independently wealthy enough to fund his Cambridge place or came from a wealthy family,
- He was wealthy enough to purchase a relatively recent innovation, a personal cine camera. (They retailed for around $70, about $1,200 at today's rates),
- He was wealthy enough to give the $125 he received from Fox to Captain Parsons,
- He would be among the cabin-class passengers and one of the signatories of the letter of condolence.

The passenger list proved extremely helpful as it recorded passengers ages and given occupations. There was only one passenger listed who fitted the bill; Frederick de Laguna, a twenty-two year old American citizen and a student.

However, Cambridge University had never had anyone of that name at the university. Neither had Oxford. Next we looked at the records of the United States Immigration Service which had recorded the details of all the passengers and crew who had arrived in New York on 10 December 1929. Frederick de Laguna had changed sex mid-Atlantic and the person who disembarked at New York was Frederica Annis Lopez de Leo de Laguna. An internet search on her lit up and put her firmly into the favourite bracket.

Born on 3 October 1906 in Ann Arbor, Michigan, Frederica (who was universally known as Freddy) became a well-regarded ethnologist, anthropologist and archaeologist. She was also a polymath of note. She had never attended Cambridge University as a student, but she was at Columbia University, and in 1928 she had travelled extensively around Europe, gaining fieldwork experience under George Grant McCurdy, the noted American anthropologist. In June 1928 she sailed to Greenland as Therkel Mathiassen's assistant in that country's first scientific archaeology expedition. She had self-financed her trip, assisted by her well-known and wealthy family. Freddy returned to the United Kingdom in 1929 and based herself at 258 Kingston Road, Teddington, Middlesex, and then on 30 November she boarded the *Baltic* at Liverpool bound for New York.

She was well known for using a trusty Leica camera to photograph the various projects she undertook and I am quite certain that she would have embraced the new medium of cinematography to assist in her work. A humanitarian at heart, I believe Freddy would have grabbed her Leica and cine cameras to record the rescue of the crew of the *Northern Light*. She could afford to buy the cine camera (probably a Kodak Model B first launched in 1925) and she could afford to give the money she got for her film to Tom Parsons. Whilst she most definitely wasn't male, didn't go to Cambridge University, nor was she a cabin-class passenger or a signatory to the letter, I believe that Chinese Whispers over the years have distorted the story a bit! I would be prepared to put a large bet on Freddy being the film-maker; but there were other candidates lurking in the passenger list who looked interesting but ticked fewer boxes.

Brenda Irene Isabelle Frances Theresa Dean Paul, was a privileged socialite born into huge wealth on 8 May 1907, and lived a pampered life in Half Moon Street, Chelsea, London. She had designs on a career in the movies and had appeared in a couple of silent films under her assumed stage name of Brenda Dean Paul. She boarded the *Baltic* in Liverpool under that name, travelling with Gerald Roberts Reitlinger. Born 2 March 1900, he gave his occupation as an artist. The pair arrived in New York 'in transit to Tahiti' via San Francisco, presumably for Reitlinger to embrace his inner Paul Gauguin there with Dean Paul as his muse. Dean Paul was certainly able to afford a cine camera and to give away her prize money, and Reitlinger would probably have had the artistic curiosity to use one; they were travelling cabin class and both signed the letter of condolence, but those are the only boxes these two tick in the hunt. Their trip to Tahiti does not appear to have been a success, as they arrived back in San Francisco on 4 March 1930 on the SS *Tahiti* from Papeete, Tahiti. They seem to have been going their separate ways in San Francisco though both returned to the United Kingdom on 11 April aboard the *Majestic* but in separate cabin-class cabins; there is no evidence that they were a couple again. Gerald may not have appreciated it at the time, but he had had a close shave. Brenda was one of the 'bright young things' of the 1930s, largely unaffected by the Depression, who continued to dash across the Atlantic with a succession of similarly entitled, louche, young men. Unfortunately, she also had a huge heroin addiction that ultimately consumed her. A number of court appearances for drug offences, a spell in Holloway Prison and any number of dishevelled and incoherent public appearances were gleefully seized on by the tabloid press of the day. Photographs of her in her last years are desperately sad. A once very beautiful woman had become a haggard shell, very unlike the Brenda I believe is pictured in the 6 December 1929 photograph taken on the deck of the *Baltic* showing Jim with most of the cabin-class passengers. I think Brenda is the woman standing behind Jim alongside the life ring that an older woman has put around her neck. Her chin is above the word 'Liverpool', she is wearing what appears to be a knitted hat and she is smiling broadly at someone or something off camera.

She died alone, a drug-addled wreck, in London on 26 July 1959. Gerald Roberts Reitlinger made a name for himself in the art world, married and divorced twice and died in Hastings in 1978. Neither Brenda nor Gerald had children. I don't think either of these two is a better candidate than Freddy.

I believe that had any of the writers of the various reports previously referred to (Brewster, Ortweiler and Major), been the film-maker they would have mentioned it in their report. They didn't–Freddy remains my stand-out favourite, though only the production of the receipt of sale to Fox Movietone will ever confirm her in that role.

Freddy enjoyed a long and productive life, dying aged ninety-eight on 6 October 2004 in Bryn Maws, Pennsylvania. She had never married, although she had at least one serious relationship, she did not have children and she outlived her siblings. She left a legacy of a huge body of work that is still an important source of reference today. As far as I have been able to establish, there are no living relatives.

The rescue film can be watched at:

https://digital.tcl.sc.edu/digital/collection/MVTN/
id/4925/rec/2

http://www.youtube.co./watch?v=ZPfELPhyAV4 (scroll
to 3:19)

Source Material

The Sinking of the Laconia–Frederick Grossmith
The Gale of 1929–Gary Collins
The Big Four of the White Star Fleet–Mark Chirnside
A History of Hull Trinity House School–D. Thompson
Exploring the Britannic–Simon Mills
The Unseen Lusitania–Eric Sauder
Bright Young People–D.J Taylor
A History of the County of York, East Riding
Fleeting Times–Henry Owen
Unpublished manuscript–Henry Owen

Other Sources and Assistance Rendered By:

Liverpool Maritime Museum
Graham Hicks–Ancestral Histories
Maritime History Archive, Memorial University of Newfoundland
Register General of Shipping and Seamen
Columbia University
University of South Carolina

University of Pennsylvania

British Film Institute (Special Collections)

Encyclopedia Titanica Forum (Northern Light/Baltic rescue)

Musée d'Histoire de Saint-Malo

Archives Maritimes–Brittany

Hull Trinity House School

Hull History Centre

Liverpool Record Office

Oxford University

Cambridge University

Southampton Library

Bute Museum

Fox Movietone Archive

United States Library of Congress

Guildhall (City of London) Library

Craig Parsons (Newfoundland)

Dave Burge

Jennifer Dutton

Carol Owen

Richard Owen

Anne-Marie Jaeger

Diane Ashton (Liverpool)

Acknowledgements

I first became fully aware of James Holland Walker in 1994 when my father published his history of the Owen family, 'Fleeting Times'. I had met Jim thirty years previously but that was as much as I knew of him. My father, before the internet and search engines transformed family-history research, uncovered the history of our family and also lifted the cover from the story of Jim's career at sea. At the time of his research in the late 1960s and early 1970s, I cannot say that it made for happy family holidays, as we children were dragged round various graveyards in Wales and Liverpool. However, today I am grateful that he did and in awe of what he managed to unearth. Everything that my father found pre-internet, I have been able to verify online. It was a remarkable feat of research by him.

Not long before he died, my father recovered three certificates awarded at the same time as three of Jim's medals, folded into many parts and lying forgotten in a distant relative's drawer. He had them restored and framed and thereafter they hung in his study where they piqued my interest, but it was not until both my parents had died that I became really interested in the man to whom those certificates had been awarded.

It became apparent that the medals Jim had been awarded had left the family some years earlier, probably disposed of by his nephew Trevor after the death of Florrie in 1978. They have passed through various hands since then, last appearing as a lot at Spink of London in July 2020. My goal is to reunite them with the three certificates and offer them to the Liverpool Maritime Museum where they, and this story, can be more widely viewed.

I owe huge thanks to my cousin Jennifer Dutton and my siblings Carol and Richard Owen who, like me, have spent too many hours on the internet and have supplied many of the photographs used in this book. My good friend, Dave Burge, recently retired, discovered he had a penchant for genealogy and assisted me in trying to establish who took the film of the *Northern Light* rescue. I doubt there is a dark corner that Dave hasn't looked in. Finally, I'd like to thank my wife Anne-Marie, for her patience and willingness to listen to me enthuse about what had come to light over the last ten months as I researched and wrote this account, and for helping me to proof and edit the manuscript. Any errors and mistakes still existing are mine.